TO OPEN ONE'S HEART
A Spiritual Path

To Open One's Heart

A Spiritual Path

Michel Evdokimov

Translated by
Anthony P. Gythiel

ST VLADIMIR'S SEMINARY PRESS
YONKERS, NEW YORK
2015

Library of Congress PCN
2014932463

Originally published in French as:
Ouvrir son cœur
© Desclée de Brouwer, 2004 and 2007

Translation Copyright © 2014

ST VLADIMIR'S SEMINARY PRESS
575 Scarsdale Road, Yonkers, NY 10707
www.svspress.com • 1-800-204-2665

ISBN 978-0-88141-489-9

PRINTED IN THE UNITED STATES OF AMERICA

Contents

PREFACE

Everything began with a few words from my grandmother, a woman of deep faith. One day she said to the little boy I was: "Search for Jesus in your heart." These words became engraved in me. All my life I incessantly looked for their significance, the dynamics of these words. They spontaneously offered a presence. From the beginning, these words were felt like a source of indispensable kindness when, at the threshold of adolescence, I lost the tenderness of a mother, this presence entirely surrounded by light, capable of leading my hesitant steps on paths full of the ambushes of a complex world.

Beyond the gloominess inherent in our human condition, beyond our weaknesses, our failings—but in God's eyes, no one is a failure, and everyone is accepted in his limitless love—this light invites one to love life, to receive the world in gratitude filled with wonder. "Be comforted! You would not be searching for me had you not found me already," Pascal said. On leaving adolescence, everyone tries to find himself. The young Christian I was hesitated between the married and the monastic state. My first experience took place in the monastery of Valaam, in the heart of Finland. The Russian monks of Old Valaam, situated on an island of Lake Ladoga, had found refuge there during World War II. An old cloistered monk lived in a cell; he was happy to receive me. He had lost an eye, and the other pierced you through like a flame. From the moment I entered the atmosphere of his cell, I learned many things from his way of being. It is he who urged me to return to the world: "Your place is over there." Other spiritual people, among whom was my own father, accompanied me on life's path. What is proper to a spiritual person—and this is still truer of a saint—is to leave a stream of light behind him. It is then possible to be carried away: to open one's heart.

To open one's heart... There are several ways of opening one's heart. The heart opens for the one who is in love. For the one who is sad, the heart is wounded. The heart conceals dizzying depths. It opens upon the abyss of the "me." It is a person's "place" in its affective, moral, and physical components. The former are also intellectual, as when someone asks God to give him "an understanding heart." They are also spiritual, as when the Lord "opened the heart" of Lydia, the purple-dye trader, listening to the preaching of Paul the apostle. Complex, rich, undulating like life, the heart eludes all rational investigation. The pages that follow are an attempt to mark out the many ways that lead to the sacred sanctuary of the person. If he desires it, every person will be able to see in them a little bit of his own experience.

1

Opening One's Heart

The Heart

Opening one's heart—why? It is done for a simple reason, it seems to me: to become enriched by the presence of the other before me, to go and meet him, or be delighted by a work of art or the beauty of the world, or lastly, to let myself be filled with God's beauty. Opening one's heart is not as simple as opening the door to one's house. "Knock and the door will be opened," the Lord says.[1] I had to; I will always need to knock, without respite, in order to be sure that the door be set ajar a little.

There is, as it were, an atmosphere of mystery in the expression "opening one's heart." The statement touches on something that is very intimate. To enable us to open ourselves to the world, we may appeal to various organs of our body. One may ask someone to open the mouth to speak, to open the ears to pay attention, to open the eyes to be vigilant. But in the expression "opening one's heart," the word *heart* is not understood only in the concrete sense of the organ. It also designates a place which, in a symbolic sense, can be opened or closed, and where many things may occur. If we consult a dictionary, we can verify that the word heart has an almost inexhaustible wealth of meanings. To say of someone that he has a heart of stone is to emphasize its closure, or to say that he has "the heart of an artichoke"[2] means that he shows an excessive

---

[1] Cf. Mt 7.7, Lk 11.9. Sometimes the author includes scriptural citations in his text, and where he does, this translation follows his practice; scriptural citations found in footnotes have been supplied in editing. In general, scriptural passages from Old Testament books are derived from Lancelot Brenton's translation of the Septuagint, and those from the New Testament books from the King James Version; in either case, the language has been updated. —Ed.

[2] "Il a un coeur d'artichaut"—a French idiom for which there is no precise English equivalent. —Ed.

openness and that he falls in love very easily. If he has a heart of gold, he is good and generous. This multiplicity of meanings shows to what extent the idea we have of a person's heart betrays his character traits metaphorically.

The first meaning of "opening one's heart" is to be open, to confide especially in a friend who then becomes a bosom friend, with whom one can speak openly. Other meanings are possible: opening one's heart may also show a compassionate or merciful heart. In this adjective, there is the word heart—*cor*, in Latin—a heart that is sensitive to the unhappiness—*miseria*, in Latin—to another's adversity. In the Gospel, Jesus asks the people to do something amazing, the impossible: "Be merciful even as your Father is merciful."[3] We will never be like the Father, but it is possible that by opening a heart of mercy, we may be similar to the divine heart, whose mercy has no limits.

Starting from the first meaning of confiding in someone, of sharing the treasures of one's heart, one may understand the opening of the heart as an opening on life, on the world, on any human situation, and also on God. Sometimes certain persons, as if struck by paralysis, are powerless to open their heart. The episode of Martha and Mary provides a good illustration of this. Some have wanted to contrast the two sisters, one propelled into action, the other into contemplation. But is contemplation not an activity implying transformation, the purification of the inner person, and is activity—be it only that of washing one's saucepans—not a moment when a person may devote oneself to one's prayer? Indeed, any activity can be transformed into prayer and does not thwart the latter in the least. What contrasts Martha to Mary is the closing or opening of the heart. When Jesus addresses himself to Martha with tenderness, by softly repeating her name, he wants to pull her out of the kitchen where she locks herself in, free her from the domestic mission she imposes on herself as if to find in it the meaning of her life. He wants to allow this activist of domestic cares to have access to a moment of graciousness, alongside her sister, and to enjoy the better part, the one thing necessary. Under the guidance of the Master at opening the heart, every disciple should work on himself to become aware of the state of openness or closure of this heart. It is self-evident that the mood varies greatly if the heart is heavy, or distraught, or elated.

---

[3] Lk 6.36.

The Heart at the Source of Life

The place of the heart, the source of the multiform expressions of life, is situated at the center of the person, in the "deep me."[4] Every human being has a body that links him to the earth from where he draws his sustenance, and to which he will return. He has a living soul that links him to the one who has breathed life into him, and to whom he will return once his earthly course is ended. But it is neither through the body, nor through the soul, that man designates this deep "me." In the spiritual tradition of the Christian East, the place of the deep "me" is the heart. The heart is endowed with a very special role. It is not an organ like the others. It must not be viewed in a purely physical sense, but as a symbolic place or, if one wishes, as an organ that is at the same time physical and spiritual. It is at the center of life, at the center of all activities, affections, thoughts, and emotions that weave the framework of existence. Like a lighthouse that sweeps the entire coast and whose mission it is to watch over it, the heart includes all the elements that make up a human being. It is identified with a person's deep me.

In ordinary language, the heart occupies a privileged place, as is attested by the multiplicity of uses of this word or of expressions in which it is integrated. As the seat of the emotions, especially those of love, it pulsates with love, or beats with indignation, even anger. The character Marius in Marcel Pagnol's trilogy is able to reproach a friend for "breaking his heart." To say of Romeo and Juliet that they were only one heart and one soul is to emphasize the vital union of their being. The heart can be the place of manifestation of a desire, a mood, a particular virtue. In the expression, "Rodrigue, do you have the heart?" it has the meaning of courage. By writing "great thoughts come from the heart," the French moralist Vauvenargues[5] places himself in the biblical tradition, where the heart is endowed with the ability to think. Why have I enumerated some varied meanings of the word heart and the multiplicity of its uses? Of all the bodily members, the heart is the only one to have acquired such status of nobility. Other internal organs—the liver, the lung, or the spleen—are hardly ever referred to, except specifically to complain about their malfunction. The heart is endowed with a preeminence that seems

---

[4] le moi profond

[5] Without giving specific citations to sources, Evdokimov often speaks of other authors and their works. We have decided to keep these mentions as they appear in the French original, with only an occasional footnote for clarification.—Ed.

to go back to the earliest of times. Is it not linked to life, by sending forth the blood in the body? Is it not equally linked to death? Of someone who has just died, one says, "His heart has stopped," as if this organ had the power of life and death. We leave the domain of metaphors, sketched above, to enter into the one where the heart comes within the scope of a profoundly existentialist view. I am alive and my heart beats. This is a certainty. The framework of my life unfolds in the beats of my heart, like the ticking of a clock.

Without a heart, the human being cannot live. Located in the center of the body, it occupies a privileged place. It is at the same time a physiological organ—like a pump, it must send blood and bring it back. It is also an organ submitted to emotions—a feeling of anger makes the heart pound. Lastly, it is an organ of the spiritual life: "You will love the Lord your God with all your heart."[6] Let us not be surprised when this polymorphous organ takes on such an importance that it is mentioned nearly a thousand times in Scripture! However, Scripture does not recognize the physiological function of the heart as an organ that regulates the circulation of the blood in the body. In the second century after Jesus Christ, the famous Greek anatomist Galen forms a very inexact idea about blood's circulation. We must wait until the eighteenth century when the English physician William Harvey discovers its mechanism. Having discovered the ingenious mechanism of this little marvel in which he contemplates the work of divine wisdom, Harvey the anatomist utters a prayer of thanksgiving: "It is in little things that the Creator is the greatest, and it is in lower beings that he sometimes lets himself be known the best."[7] Is it not surprising that the muscle represents the only organ not to be invaded by a proliferation of malignant cells? No one has ever suffered from a cancer of the heart.

Thus, the heart is at the same time a physiological organ indispensable to life, the seat of emotions and of the depth of being. It is also the symbolic place of encounter between the human being and God, the place where one runs the risk of destiny. This preeminence of the heart is omnipresent in Scripture where it adorns almost every page. Consequently, it has marked the foundation of our Judeo-Christian civilization. In Scripture, the question is not only that of a contrite, broken heart, or,

---

[6] Mt 22.37, Mk 12.30, Lk 10.27; cf. Dt 6.5.

[7] As quoted by P. Ide, in *Pour une civilisation du cœur* (Paris: Éditions de l'Emmanuel, 2000), p. 93.

conversely, one that is gladdened (for example, by wine!); it is a question of strengthening the heart, of guarding it or of turning it away, of probing it or of following its inclinations... In these situations of life, on which sometimes depends the destiny of a being whose heart leans toward the good or toward evil, toward salvation or perdition, it appears like a vital organ placed in the deepest "me." It designates the very center of my person, where the person consults, makes decisive choices, devotes himself to reflection or turns toward God. The heart marks the boundary of this inner space where the encounter with the Creator takes place.

Some Misfortunes of the Heart in the West

In the West, St Augustine is the one who meditated the most on the heart. Almost all of the biblical meanings of this word are reflected in his pen, especially in his *Confessions*. There, it frequently designates the secret intimacy of the human being, "the inner room" where the drama of existence is played out, or conversion and salvation. The heart is an "unfathomable" abyss, that of the saints being expanded still by charity, and God not merely resides there, but he walks in it.

In the times that follow the century of the bishop of Hippo, the heart is far from occupying the central place in piety. In its immense effort to make the mystery accessible to human reason, medieval scholastic theology tends rather not to trust anything that depends upon the heart. However, in its practice, if not its theology, the West is far from having lost its connection to the heart. The first one to ask himself the question of what role the heart plays in man's inner world, even to the point of making it the foundation of his anthropology, is Pascal.

When reading his *Pensées*, one cannot fail to be struck by the abundance of biblical quotations where the word "heart" is found. As in Augustine, the heart marks the dynamism of the soul, the deep movements of the inner life. Sometimes on a very personal note, Pascal paints a somber picture of the heart: "How hollow and foul is the heart of man!" Bent over the edge of this "cistern" (the image is taken from Jeremiah), he casts glances filled with dread: "I see my abyss of pride, of curiosity, of concupiscence... this infinite cave can be filled only by God himself." In the spaces of his heart, St Augustine enjoyed peace and sweetness, while Pascal turned away in disgust from this "hateful me."[8]

---

[8] ce moi haïssable

In the thought of this great philosopher, the heart sets itself up as an organ of knowledge, as in Scripture. "We know the truth not only through our reason, but also through our heart." Would he humiliate reason? Such is not the intention of this great scientific genius who, in a dignified manner, wants to prevent reason from going beyond its proper sphere: "What a long way it is between knowing God and loving him." "This is what faith is: God perceived by the heart, not by the reason!" This metaphor denotes all of man in his natural as well as supernatural principle. Here the theologian places himself in the Pauline tradition: "It is by believing in the heart that one arrives at justice." Fine psychological observations let an insightful observer of human behavior shine through with very modern echoes: "The heart has its reasons of which Reason knows nothing." The dark content of the subconscious underlies the conduct of people. Their reasonable powers, confined to a limited role, very frequently undergo the influence of the heart's inner turmoil. After St Augustine, only the East was to maintain the tradition of the heart. The West was to distance itself from this rich tradition until it saw in the heart only the seat of sensibility. However, in this philosophical desert, there is a refreshing island, namely the thoughts of Pascal.

In the days following the death of Pascal, the conflict between Bossuet and Fénelon broke out concerning the quietism of Madame Guyon. Fénelon extols a mode of persuasion through feeling and the heart, without, however, scorning the sovereign freedom of reason. The victory of the Eagle of Meaux over the bishop of Cambrai is that of a Catholicism based on the authority of the hierarchy, and unconcerned about the impulses of the heart. With this, mystical literature was excluded until the nineteenth century.

With the classical school, the heart as seat of the mythology of love suffers an eclipse so as to be considered with reason only an organ of flesh and blood like the others. Descartes maintains that "the seat of the passions is not in the heart." In the eighteenth century, we witness a sterilizing of the heart by Sade, Laclos, etc. in the erotic games of a society that knows how to die with panache but cultivates the refinements of lust. Furthermore, this century of "lights" wants to promote a pure and unyielding rationalism. This consecration of Reason "is the work of a France that loses its head only because its heart has been led astray."[9] Some break with this ascendancy of progress and reason. They feel

---

[9] *Le Cœur*, Études Carmélitaines (Paris: Desclée de Brouwer, 1950), p. 372.

quivering in themselves an intimate, secret life, which they are sometimes tempted to bring into the light of day, as Rousseau does in his *Confessions*. One then finds an inflation of the "I," a listening to the language of the heart, thereby opening a great vein of romantic inspiration. Sometimes one cultivates melancholy in the heart. It is a vague sentiment, the source of a suffering that is all the more acute as its cause remains imprecise...

> It rains in my heart
> As it rains on the town
> By far the worst pain
> Without hatred, or love,
> Yet no way to explain
> Why my heart feels such pain!

Verlaine declares correctly.

In the twentieth century, the atrophy of the heart is brutally felt. Communism abhors what falls under the heart, feelings, even when it fools itself by borrowing "inverse" concepts from Christianity: "paradise"—but on earth—"brotherhood" among the peoples—but brothers without a Father. Apart from the totalitarian ideologies, the wilting of the heart can be perceived in the tendency of the modern period to aim for efficiency, of letting oneself be captivated by the mirages of technocracy, of the various media such as the Internet, the entertainments of omnipresent television, where man, bombarded by images, is seized by what is external to him, diverted from the great mysteries of his deep life. The great number of psychic diseases—are they not a sign of an inadequacy in governing one's inner kingdom? The violence of the suburbs, is it not the sign of a youth that is badly loved or not at all? The repression of the heart goes together with a collapse of tenderness, of femininity—not that of stars or of models—in a brutal world, devoted to productivity and the money chase.

Sensitive souls sometimes happen to return to the heart, and to its ability to pierce the mystery of beings and things. The Little Prince is informed about this path by the fox: "Here is my secret," the fox says. "It is very simple: one sees well only with the heart. What is essential is invisible to the eyes." The famous phrase of St Augustine in his *Confessions* is always real: "Our heart will be restless until it rests in Thee." In a biblical language, he expresses the passionate impulse of his fervent piety. When a great spiritual author wants to let the infinite love of God be understood, he resorts to the heart metaphorically: "It is difficult to represent the Father to ourselves. We will perhaps come near the truth if we think of the Father as of a heart, each beat of which is like an infinite act of love."[10]

Moreover, the heart is linked to the blood on which a heavy interdiction lies from the depths of the ages. For the Semites, blood is life. Now, for a people that crosses a desert infested with wild animals under a torrid sun, and settles in the land of Canaan, inhabited by hostile and belligerent peoples, life must be preserved at all costs. The taboo of blood makes one impure.

St John of Kronstadt

The heart is the eye of the human being. The purer it is, the quicker, farther, and clearer it can see. But with God's saints this spiritual eye is refined, even during their lifetime, to the highest degree of purity possible for man, and after their death, when they have become united to God, through God's grace, it becomes still clearer and wider in the limits of its vision. Therefore the saints see very clearly, widely, and far: they see our spiritual wants; they see and hear all those who call upon them with their whole hearts—that is, those whose mental eyes are fixed straight upon them, and are not darkened or dimmed when so fixed by unbelief and doubt; in other words, when the eyes of the heart of those who pray meet the eyes of those they call upon. This is a mysterious vision.

In the parable of the good Samaritan, if the priest and the Levite do not deign to bring help to the man lying on the side of the road, it is perhaps because, by going to the Temple to fulfill there a sacred function, they do not want to make themselves impure. Only the brave Samaritan dares defy the taboo of blood and brings help to the wounded man. It is known that Jews consume kosher meat, that is, of animals killed according to the rules of the Mosaic Law to stem the flow of blood. The flow of blood on certain days of the month makes a woman impure. In this sense, the heart that pumps blood is well set at the source of the organic, physical life.

As soon as Abel is murdered, the voice of innocent blood cries to God and awakens his compassion. Beyond death, the blood continues

---

[10] Lev Gillet, *Notre Père* (Paris: Éditions du Cerf and Beirut: Éditions An-Nour, 2012), p. 15.

to express life; it has the power of speech, and it demands atonement. In the features of this innocent shepherd killed by his brother, some have seen a face that prefigured that of Christ. He too was the image of the good shepherd; he too was killed by his brothers, but his blood was shed for them of his own free will. Blood receives a new connotation. It is no longer the blood that signs the death warrant, but the blood that gives life and which saves it. The people of the Old Covenant are awaiting the one who is sent—the Messiah—by God. His innocent blood, shed for all, will seal a New Alliance with humanity.

Mastering One's Heart

The heart, a physical organ, is the object of great solicitude. Some try to eradicate cardio-vascular diseases that are a cause of high mortality in France. Others devote themselves to athletic activity, by imposing on themselves a life of hygiene. All this is done for a practical goal. One encounters many young people at the age of adolescence—or beyond— who feel they are handicapped by states of emotionalism, of hypersensitivity, and of anguish. On the physical level, the heart rhythm accelerates. As a last resort, some try to control these states by resorting to all types of stimulants: tobacco, which offers a very ephemeral relaxation; drugs, which can lead to a worse degradation than the trouble; love relations which in their emotional fragility bring no stability. The various methods of psychotherapy, antidepressants or anxiety-solving drugs, which are consumed in high numbers in France, may calm the symptoms without ever eradicating the root of the problem. In the worst of cases, such conditions may lead to suicide, and the number of suicides is climbing. Suicide is also practiced in Christian circles, even though they are bringers of hope in announcing the Good News. Others turn to techniques of the Far East. The bodily discipline of yoga, with the holding of breath, sometimes gives rise to a great mastery over the emotions.

In society, the image of God, in particular that of a loving Father, becomes greatly blurred. Since the events of 1968 that weakened the student movement—even all of society—the concept of fatherhood has been deeply degraded. Could one of the causes of violence, of indifference, of malaise, not be linked directly to a deep anxiety about the absence of true fatherhood? Many people in a world where "it is forbidden to forbid" (the slogan that was all the rage in 1968!), take refuge in what the world can offer in consumer goods, a diffuse hedonism, or a lack of inner discipline. The landmarks have been blown up.

The Russian novelist Dostoevsky has brilliantly illustrated this lack of fatherhood freely undertaken and accepted in his great metaphysical novel, *The Brothers Karamazov*. Fyodor, the father, is a grotesque buffoon, who attracts sarcasm to himself. The oldest, Dimitri—his name derives from Demeter, the goddess of harvests—is a man of instinct and of the soil, of the vital powers, a man of flesh and blood. The second, Ivan, is a skeptical intellectual, removed from concrete realities, and in revolt against the state of the world. The third, Alyosha, is the only one to have a father, not according to the flesh, but according to the spirit. It is Zosima, the staretz, who urges him to leave the monastery where he is only a novice, to go into the world and take care of his brothers. Finally, the fourth brother, Smerdiakov, the bastard, the fruit of a rape committed by the old Fyodor upon a somewhat simple-minded woman, following a stupid bet, is the architect of a patricide committed with the more or less silent consent of the two older brothers. The novelist writes down this terrible sentence that particularly attracted the attention of Freud, "Who has never wanted to kill his father?" In this novel are found the great tendencies of humankind: the propensity for instinct, for the cerebral, the spiritual life, and the forces of darkness that break down the individual. In this novel, the death of the father, however undignified he might be, is symbolic of the death of Adam in Paradise at the moment when Adam surrendered to the desire to be "like God." It is also symbolic of the supposed absence of the Father in the contemporary world. The sons are orphans. The absence of authority forces them to undergo the hard apprenticeship of freedom which, in the worst of cases, leads them to construct totalitarian systems where perverted freedom turns into its opposite, the subservience of peoples.

However, the human being is not deprived of his religious, inalienable foundation, even though he may not be aware of it. The phenomenon of these quasi-sacred ritual liturgies called rave-parties shows that one can dance day and night, the ears deafened by decibels, the eyes blinded by flashes, without seeing the face of an eventual partner, without a heart-to-heart, or even a body-to-body counterpart. What hides this drift, all moorings broken, toward the islands of loneliness? Projected outside himself—outside his heart—the young dancer is snapped up by the sounds, the light, the human mass around him that rises and falls, and undulates like a sea. What thirst for communion pushes thousands of young people to gather together to sacrifice to the rhythms of techno music? What a thirst also for the Father in whom they could put their hopes, their joy of living?

The silence of God does not mean absence. The seekers of the absolute are legion, even though they make no noise. For them, the marks are no longer given; they are to be sought. A short time ago, a university student, a fierce disciple of dialectic materialism, confided that he felt happy when he found himself in his own interiority. As one might think, he had found the path of his heart, where the great revelations of life occur. A woman student who thought she was "indifferent," ended up giving herself to Christ and asked to be baptized, after an in-depth reading of literary works marked by the faith of their authors.

The Heart at the Center of the Person

In such a context, to evoke the heart, this place related symbolically to the physical heart, is to propose a pedestal on which a person may rebuild or renew himself. On what then can I base myself to ensure the stability of my being? The answers to this question can vary. Sometimes we ask ourselves: what is the quality of life that surrounds me, where does it come from, and where does it go? Believers refer to the Bible which tells us that the human being has been fashioned, modeled from the soil: "For dust you are, and unto dust shall you return."[11] These words send a shiver down the spine. They reduce the human body after death to so little! Now God breathes his spirit into the nostrils molded from clay, and this "person of clay" becomes a living soul. This gesture is fascinating. It signifies that life is a gift that comes from elsewhere, a vital breath that animates a being from birth on and accompanies one until the last breath. The miracle of existence!

A prayer that opens all the liturgical offices of the Orthodox Church is addressed to the Holy Spirit in these words: "Treasury of good things and Giver of Life: come and abide in us…" The Holy Spirit not only gives people this immense gift of life, but what is more, he can, if the heart opens up to him, make his dwelling in us, enter therein as a person. Then these "temples of the Holy Spirit" of which St Paul speaks are built. They conceal the treasures of divine grace. The one who dares wound, torture, or destroy this temple undermines the Holy Spirit himself whose mysterious guest he is. Man is not the master of life, the source of which is somewhere else. He may well be experienced in bioethics, he may well

---

[11] Gen 3.14, 19.

manipulate male and female cells in test tubes, but the miracle that causes the spark of life to grow does not come under his jurisdiction. When in the prayer to the Holy Spirit we ask him "to make his dwelling in us," that is a way of telling him: I open my heart as well as I can, and I am ready to receive you. Opening one's heart means to love.

This openness of heart must be taken seriously. The Lord invites us to it, quoting the words of Isaiah: "The people honor me only with lip-service, while their hearts are far from me."[12] The mysticism of the heart, this openness of the deep "me" to a mysterious reality beyond the person, consists precisely in not being satisfied by mumbling prayers with the tip of the tongue, or by practicing rituals to get them over with. Christ castigates this lukewarm and hypocritical faith. Let us hope that the heart of man comes closer to God, and his lips praise him in truth! All true prayer descends into the depths of the heart. A long and patient apprenticeship is needed to free oneself from the enslaving seductions of the world, to maintain the spirit closely linked to the heart or enclosed in it. Emotions and impulses are then mastered peacefully and, more precisely, it is the divine Spirit that, having made his dwelling in man, carries out this mastery in him.

The Gospel earnestly exhorts us to pray: "Watch and pray, for you do not know the day or the hour."[13] Prayer is a familiar occupation for the believer who wishes to deepen his faith or make his life a prayer. It introduces a spark of eternity into the heart. The last moment of our existence, when it is to end, remains hidden from us. For some, it will be a fall into nothingness, and the idea of this may be the source of a cruel anxiety. For others, it will be the entrance into another reality, that of eternal life, that of a Father of mercy always ready to welcome those who, at the end of their suffering, turn to him. He has indeed welcomed the prodigal son who, deprived of everything and tottering at the edge of the abyss, had the courage to return to the one to whom he owed his life. This is perhaps the meaning of prayer: to chase away the hideous mask of death, of despair.

To open one's heart, one needs a counterpart, an intimate friend on earth, or a friend in heaven. The vigilance required by Christ—"Watch and pray"—does not concern only the last moment. There are many other deaths, such as this succession of little deaths to the self: miniature,

---

[12] Is 29.13.

[13] Cf. Mt 25.13.

victorious deaths—a mastery over selfishness, enmity, narcissism, spiritual lethargy, inner turmoil—of everything that is a cause of suffering in my relationships with the other, and which does not leave me at peace. Montaigne sought peace in the art of dying well, but it is given especially by the one who incarnates peace in his person: "my own peace I give you; a peace which the world cannot give, this is my gift to you."[14] Now, society does not teach the art of dying well. Nonetheless, one speaks a great deal about death. It is found everywhere, in the news, in movies, in virtual reality. It is put on as a spectacle, as if to exorcise the anxiety it provokes, as if to postpone the moment when one realizes that man is mortal, and that this is no longer virtual. They let people die at the hospital, sometimes in a mournful lonesomeness. The custom of the funeral wake where friends and family surrounding the body of the deceased quietly meditated upon their own death has fallen into disuse. And with this, a little hope leaves in shreds... The ancient Stoics, and Montaigne with them, proclaim that the aim of philosophy is learning how to die. This is unquestionably a noble exploit. The Christian faith, conveying hope, brings a bit of hope into the matter. "The one who eats my flesh and drinky my blood dwells in me, and I in him."[15] Is this not a way of saying that in the eucharistic act, it is already given to us here below to receive a foretaste of life eternal?

Montaigne further adds, "What a marvelously vain, diverse, and billowy subject is man." The word "billowy"[16] evokes that which is mobile, capricious, continually changing. Always fleeting and diverse, man has a hard time reflecting. Moreover, so has the world in which he moves about. The rapid evolutions of techniques, the change of living conditions, the development of the means of entertainment—in the Pascalian sense where man devotes himself to entertainment to forget that he is mortal—are not made to give a serene stability to this fleeting human. According to a survey made in the United States, the average American will have spent fifteen years in front of his television set! Really hooked to the little screen, projected outside himself, he will have left his inner "me" shot through by thousands of images, emotions, and situations. It is not a question of publicly condemning technologies, entertainments, or the virtual spaces which people will always have to learn how to master, but of appreciating to what extent many among them are fascinated, if not

[14] Cf. Jn 14.27.

[15] Jn 6.56.

[16] ondoyant

fashioned, by these media. Certain recent studies show indeed to what extent a psychological make-up that is more or less frail can be unhinged by violent movies. When they are badly lived, or consumed excessively, the means of entertainment tear man away from his inner life.

The Heart-to-Heart Communion

All of us have to learn about the person, that is to say how to arrive at knowledge of self and knowledge of others. This is a noble task to achieve in existence. Socrates had already assigned the famous "know thyself" (*gnothi seauton*) as the aim of philosophy. Christ invites people to explore the depths of the "me" when he asks them to search for the Kingdom, because, he says, "It is within you."[17] This phrase is paradoxical, for we think of the Kingdom in terms of space, of an extrinsic place, and not in terms of the spiritual life, of communion with God. On his cross, the good thief proclaims to Christ: "Lord, remember me when you come into your kingdom." He receives this reply: "Today you will be with me in paradise."[18] Paradise or the Kingdom is to be with Christ, in communion with him. Christ urges us to search for the Kingdom, to search for this mysterious reality of the Kingdom that, once discovered, will make us fully human and will give us fullness of life.

With self-knowledge there is the knowledge of the neighbor whom Christ asks us to love, and, even for good measure, to love him as we love ourselves. I have always been struck by the fact that the kiss of peace in the Liturgy—unfortunately, in the Orthodox Church, only the clergy share it with one another—is exchanged just before the proclamation of the Creed. Before we utter a word about God, before we discern his mystery in order to know him as much as is possible, we make a gesture of love. Thus, love of neighbor elevates us to the love of God, just as the love of God turns us toward the neighbor.

One cannot have an idea of what a person is unless one represents him in communion with others. This communion is not synonymous with "fusion," as in collectivism, where the mass always wins out over the individual. The person has an absolute value. And as such, a person is irreplaceable, irreducible. A person alone would be an island, lost on the immense ocean of life. With parents, friends, schoolmasters, colleagues at work, a network of subtle relationships, more or less intense, is being

[17] Cf. Lk 7.21.

[18] Lk 23.42, 43.

woven. These relationships control the opening—or the closing!—of the heart to favor this communion without which life becomes impossible. A bishop was once asked the following question: "What is the moment, the place, or the person that is the most important of my life?" He answered: "It is the present moment I am living, the place where I am, and the person before me with whom I am speaking. If that person is there, is it not because the Lord has placed him on my way, and has made this meeting possible?"

In the Gospel according to John, we find amazing words in which the most intimate union that can exist between God and man is expressed: "If anyone loves me, he will keep my words, and my Father will love him; and we will come to him and we will make our abode with him" (Jn 14.23). What does this expression, "make our abode with him" mean? Perhaps it means to dwell in the place where he dwells. But certain spiritual persons agree in thinking that this expression designates a person's inwardness, and, in the first place, his place of choice, the heart. The same idea is found in another passage. Christ commands us to go and pray in our room, after closing the door, for there is the Father, in secret. This room can indeed be interpreted as the place where we spend part of our life, but also as the place of the heart. Closing the door then means becoming deaf, insensitive to all solicitations, seductions, and temptations of the world... An example is found of the yogi who, sitting on the step of his house, remained uncomplainingly immersed in his mediations, while a noisy festive procession passed before his eyes. Closing the door is to be entirely present before the Father, in a humble, earthly nakedness, attentive to the dialogue that is about to be established.

The Combat between Light and Darkness

Are we always able to receive the divine in us? When we invite friends to our home, we clean the living room, adorn it with flowers, make it as beautiful and welcoming as possible, to make them feel the warmth of the friendship with which we want to surround them. Is the same true also for the divine guest? How do we accept him in the abode of our heart? When he knocks at the door, the living room is perhaps in disorder, the floor has not been swept for several days, garments lie around on the furniture, the windows have not been washed, and the light is poor. How could the one who is the Light put up with such poverty? But there is much worse. In the back of the living room a darkened corridor opens areas where the dust of years has accumulated, and where there is a rancid smell that grips us by the throat. Certain pieces are condemned; the lock has been rusting for ages. What shameful secrets hide in these places? What skeletons are concealed in the closets?

"The light shines in the darkness, and the darkness has not comprehended it" (Jn 1.5)—or has not received it, the Apostle John writes. What does such darkness mean? Is it the inner darkness that reveals the somber face of sin at work in the world, at work in the heart of people when they turn away from the one who said: "I am the light of the world"?[19] In this case, the heart becomes the receptacle, or the garbage dump of what cannot be mentioned. Its depths hide the unvoiced feelings, the frustrations—everything that was bad or unloved—and also, whether one is aware of this or not, the suffering of being a sinner. A great saint said that if one gathered all the sins of all humanity, they would form only one drop of water in the ocean of God's mercy.

The modern era arrogantly challenges the notion of "sin"—a challenge that neither questions sin as such, nor above all suppress it! In the court of justice the general tendency consists in accumulating excuses to explain, even justify, the behavior of a defendant. He may have suffered from an unbalanced mind, an unjust social situation, unworthy parents… One must at any price rationalize what depends upon an irrational mystery, evil. A simple victim of elements he no longer controls, the criminal of all kinds is deprived of any type of freedom. He has perhaps undergone the weight of social determinism, hereditary or other, but, ultimately, a part of his being remains irreducible.

One relaxes the bridle to the passions in the rapture of a freedom one imperiously claims and which one believes to be unlimited. And see how this freedom, having become mad, turns against those who believed they had mastered it. All the revolutions based on a limitless freedom to start with—but this time does not last—result in despotism, a limitless tyranny. When Abbé Pierre talks with a group of young people on television on the depth of the commitment of love, and suggests to them as an infallible contraceptive—self-discipline to fight against AIDS—he is booed. AIDS increases its ravages, human eros remains wounded by love games reduced to instinctive impulses. Freud saw in love and death, *eros* and *thanatos*, the bi-polarity where the life of man is enacted or becomes unraveled. Christ shows us that love is as strong as death; only he is able

---

[19] Jn 8.12, 9.5.

to rout the latter. Christ dies on the Cross in an ultimate gesture of love.

It is time once again to honor inner discipline, effort, and prayer, to let a little bit of light shine. Life is a fight between light and darkness. The heart is in the fray of this fight. Man can be submitted to various conditionings. The latter can illumine a particular behavior, but they will never exhaust the totality of the human being. Man always keeps a bit, a spark of liberty in his innermost heart of hearts. This is why the Apostle Luke writes that "the good man draws good things from the good treasure of his heart, and the evil man draws evil things from the evil treasure of his heart."[20] As the dynamic center of the person, the heart allows one to identify the latter under its veil of light, or of darkness.

If it is accepted that the heart designates the deep "me," the most intimate spot of the person, then we may begin to listen to what it has to say to guide our life, and to let it unfold freely. It is good to settle in the heart.

The Wounds of the Heart

In the sinful condition that is proper to it, that is, in its very nature, the heart of every human being is a wounded heart. Engraved in the heart, each one bears the wounds of life, of a bad education, even a catechesis from which a false representation of God emerges, of God as a terrible Father, angered, ready to punish his rebellious creature. The heart is ambivalent. It is at the same time linked to the body, of which it is the driving force, and to the soul—the psyche—this principle of life, conscious and unconscious, planted in each one of us. One day, a man goes to a priest to confess that his marriage is in a bad way. There are extramarital relations, and his wife, to whom he remains attached, spends entire days confined to bed with a painful back problem. To the question of whether he happens to talk with his wife, if words are exchanged between them to unravel the situation, the answer is that there is nothing of this. They no longer have anything to say to one another. The priest then suggests that since words no longer pass between the couple, it is the woman's sick back that speaks, that cries out its suffering of not being recognized and an inability to express this. The closing of the heart has brought on a blockage of words and a withering of the feelings that give rise to physical pain. The one piece of advice to give to this man was to tell him to go back to his wife and ask her for forgiveness.

[20] Lk 6.45.

Forgiveness is the surest way to rediscover the path of the heart with regard to the self as to the neighbor. Sometimes, forgiveness appears within reach. Our heart overflows with love for our surroundings, for all of humanity, except… for that certain person with whom it is impossible to get along, since she is so unbearable, bad-tempered, and detestable. In this case, forgiving is out of the question. And yet, she is the one whom God paradoxically puts on our path. Only she can allow us to gain the upper hand, the decisive victory over pride, and to make our way to holiness. Love of the enemy is the touchstone of our faith.

One day, a priest carries the last rites to a lady on her deathbed, and during confession he asks her whether her heart is at peace, whether she has truly forgiven her entourage. She replies that she is at peace with everyone, except with her son-in-law; she had sworn she would never forgive him on account of an insult he had inflicted on her. The priest replies: "Then, I cannot give you communion. Go and be reconciled to your son-in-law. I will return in two hours. Pray that you are still alive at that moment." After two hours, and after being reconciled in good and proper form with her son-in-law, the lady rejoined her Lord, her soul at peace. In the case of this pardon obtained *in extremis*, the heart's turn-about was surprising. Almost always, this requires considerable time. Scripture writes about stiff-necked people, whom it is not easy to bend, to soften under the millstone of humility. The transformation of the heart of stone into a heart of flesh as God evokes it through the mouth of the prophet[21] is done in little steps. By flowing drop by drop on the hard rock, the water takes centuries to pierce it, but it always gains the upper hand.

Sometimes words of discouragement are heard: I do not feel any progress in my spiritual life! Nevertheless, we are poor judges of our spiritual state. Persevering in the faith implies not letting the heart drown in despair. The spiritual life stretches out in time, imperceptibly. However, there are criteria that are the result of prayer and that St Paul notes: patience, peace, love, and joy. A joy born from the announcement of the Good News, joy that was radiant on the faces of the first disciples of Christ… People of our time sometimes look sad. All one has to do is to watch them in the subway, in the streets. Sometimes a simple smile is enough to make them change their face. A Russian novelist writes that a person's character is expressed in the way he laughs, an open, spontaneous laughter that rings out into a joyful sparkle. One of the Desert

---

[21] Ezek 36.26.

Fathers adds: "Do not talk to me about monks that never laugh; they are not serious!" Another Russian author adds that one day Satan will be yawning with boredom and in his opened mouth he would then swallow the entire world…

Joy and suffering alternate in every human life. Wounds should be dressed. Are we aware of the sufferings we inflict on account of sin?

St Isaac the Syrian

And what is a merciful heart? He replied: "The heart's burning for all creation, for human beings, for birds and animals, and for demons and everything there is. At the recollection of them and at the sight of them his eyes gush forth with tears owing to the force of the compassion which constrains his heart, so that, as a result of its abundant sense of mercy, the heart shrinks and cannot bear or examine any harm or small suffering of anything in creation. For this reason he offers up prayer with tears at all times, even for irrational animals, and for the enemies of truth, and for those who harm him, for their preservation and forgiveness. As a result of the immense compassion infused in his heart without measure—like God's—he even does this for reptiles."

The tongue indulges in speaking evil of someone, and behold! the heart retracts. Only a recourse to a request for forgiveness offers the balm capable of comforting it. To bind up the wounds of the heart, there is the great Physician, Christ, and the supreme remedy, the Eucharist. "So then, if you are bringing your offering to the altar, and there you remember that your brother has something against you, leave your offering there before the altar, and go and be reconciled with your brother first" (Mt 5.23–24).

War is everywhere. Examples in the world are plenty. Recourse to violence causes counter-violence in an endless spiral where the triumph of some brings about humiliation in others. Only the recourse to forgiveness—and forgiveness is the supreme power—can break this infernal spiral. What seems impossible to obtain when populations are at stake, is not impossible when it concerns persons. A peaceful man capable of asking for forgiveness unleashes a dynamic of peace around him. Examples like that of the German leaders asking for forgiveness from the victims of the Holocaust, the pope for violence exercised in the name of the Church, or the patriarch of Russia for the persecutions of the Old Believers, deserve to be especially emphasized. Peace in the world finds its starting point in the peace that reigns in the heart of every person.

We should think of Christ not as a judge ready to condemn or punish every breach of the Law, but as "a physician of souls and bodies." The prayer that comes before receiving communion in the Liturgy of St John Chrysostom specifies: "Not unto judgment nor unto condemnation be my partaking of thy Holy Mysteries, O Lord, but unto the healing of soul and body." The Eucharist expresses the administration of this spiritual medicine. Christ has come to earth not in a spirit of anger, not to offer himself as a sacrifice in order to appease the Father's anger—a Father who is Love!—but to save, that is, to heal people of their sins and to open for them the ways of love. The Gospel abounds with innumerable examples where the crippled and the maimed are set aright, the blind regain their sight and the mute begin to speak.

A new life circulates among people, a reflection of the love of the One the Father sends, not to judge, but to save the world. The Father did not want the death of his Son, as if he demanded the offering of a human sacrifice to appease his divine fury, roused by the disobedience of his creature. Such a concept is pagan. It does not fit the image of a merciful Father as he is revealed to be by his Son through this exhortation: "Be merciful just as your Father is merciful" (Lk 6.36). Christ went willingly to his death. He has never sought suffering as such. He does not evade what he must accomplish, for only a God can overcome death by death and free people from the fatality that has weighed on them for so long. For this, he goes through a night of suffering in the garden of Gethsemane, during which he experiences an extreme sense of being forsaken: living the anguished feeling of being abandoned by the love of the Father. After surviving this moment of horror, as a man, he can confront the Passion and the descent into Hell, in all his divine power. He forgives the executioners, because they do not know what they are doing. Indeed, they have not opened in themselves the paths of their hearts, the ones that lead to love and not to hatred. These are the very paths we are given to walk on in joy and hope so that, every day, each time we turn away from limitless Love, we do not crucify Christ once more.

The Eucharist is often characterized as "a remedy unto immortality." It is indeed a communion with the Lamb of God that takes away the sins of the world and heals man's spiritual diseases. The reconciliation with one's brother that is asked urgently before one presents one's offering to God brings to our attention the need to have peace reign in us and around us. A priest had been jailed for several years in the prisons of a totalitarian country. He had come out of there filled with light. He had never prayed so hard during his entire life, he said. He had transfigured the time that seemed endless to other detainees, a time of revolt and despair, into a time of communion with God, and, in spite of terrible suffering, into a time of great availability toward all... In a monastery close to a large city lived a monk confessor who had received the gift of tears. He wept over the sins of those who came to confess to him, tears of "com-passion" in the etymological sense of "suffering with," tears that stream and wash away the people's sins.

The Eucharist is also identified with love. This word is heavy with various connotations. Here it can be taken only in its true depth where it is linked to life eternal. The source of all love is in God. In the Eucharist, we partake of the body and blood of the One who takes upon himself our deaths to restore us to the true life through his resurrection. Love does not come automatically; one should prepare one's heart to love. The love of a mother for her children seems something natural, innate. Even so, a mother of four children one day gave this testimony: "In my youth, I was never loved. My father never put me on his knees, my mother never caressed me. I am very afraid that I do not know how to pass on to my children what I never received." A young girl in full adolescence is brutally separated from her mother, carried off by a painful disease. Since her father had left, the girl finds that she is alone, without being able to say goodbye. But one thing sustains her: knowing that her mother, still living, continues to pray for her in the light of Christ. When she herself turns toward Christ, she recognizes her mother, in him. A sad idea is circulating these days: love is a beautiful flame, but it does not last. But is the heart not able to be faithful and to deepen the object of its love during an entire life, even when the latter does not cease getting longer? A character from a Russian novel claims that a man who has loved a single woman in his life knows more about women than all the Don Juans or the Casanovas of the earth gathered together. What is a love that has no resonance in eternity? Love is stronger than death, Scripture says.

2

HEALING THE BROKEN-HEARTED

Divine Words and the Human Heart

An important stage in my development was the awareness that those whose heart was broken may find themselves face-to face with God who, by willingly ascending the Cross, has, on his part, allowed his heart to be broken. God too is vulnerable. At the dawn of history, when God is reconciled to man in Noah, the redactor of Genesis writes: "The Lord said in his heart, 'I will never again I curse the ground'" (Gen 8.21). Compassion, set in motion, will win out over everything else. If I can speak to God, if I can love him, is it not because he has a limitless capacity for love, the emblem of which is also the heart? Speaking to God heart-to-heart then becomes possible.

All those who are familiar with reading the sacred Scriptures cannot fail to be impressed by the abundance of passages where the word "heart" is used. No fewer than a thousand times may be enumerated. This tells us to what extent, in Scripture, this organ occupies a place of choice in the various aspects of human life… It is possible to approach this "swaying, different" being which man is through one of the many facets of his personality: rationality, sensitivity, and sexuality. Scripture, for its part, emphasizes the heart. It makes of it the linchpin of its anthropology. Thus, God addresses himself to the heart of man. He speaks to it to awaken it to the divine life, occasionally to rebuke it when it turns away from his paths, to cause it to become aware of the mission the Most High has assigned to it on earth. The heart serves as a sounding box where the Word descends in the depths of the person. Mary, the sister of Martha, echoes the "Hear, O Israel"—*Shᵉma' Israel*—the one who, sitting at the feet of Jesus, "heard" his words. To open one's heart is, therefore, to enter into a first approach to faith, in an attentive listening to the dialogue about to develop between God and the human being.

In his commentary on the parable of the sower, Jesus says that the Word is "sown" in the hearts. The sowing occurs in this symbolic earth that is sometimes unproductive, frequently infertile, obstructed with undergrowth, where the grain perishes; but sometimes easily worked, and fertile, where it bears abundant fruit. Nothing can be hidden from the gaze of God who knows the hearts of men. In a long dispute with Pharisees, where the question dealt with blasphemy against the Spirit that will not be forgiven, Jesus teaches, "Out of the abundance of the heart the mouth speaks. A good man out of the good treasure of his heart brings forth good things, and an evil man out of his evil treasure brings forth evil things" (Mt 12.34–35[1]). Far from being inert, the heart possesses laws, a proper dynamic, susceptible of orienting human choices according to its degree of openness or closure when confronted with the realities of existence. Is it not the worst thing is not to say to someone: You have no heart! This is to make him lower than an animal, which, like a faithful dog, can sometimes show that it has a heart…

The high opinion Scripture has of the central place occupied by the heart in human life, as it has been decreed by God, leads it to consider that the hearts of people form an integral part of God's plan for the salvation of humankind. At the end of his prophetic book, Malachi predicts the coming of the Messiah, whom he portrays under the features of Elijah. This Messiah is charged with "turning the heart of the fathers to their children, and the heart of the children to their fathers" (Mal 4.6). Reconciling the hearts of the fathers to the hearts of the children is to make possible their conversion, to reestablish understanding between generations, the union needed for the advent of the Kingdom.

At the opening of the Gospel according to Luke, Zechariah, the high priest in the service of the Temple, receives the visit of an angel, who repeats the prophecy of Malachi; but this time the one sent by God is no longer Elijah: it is John the Baptist, the very son of Zechariah. With the power of Elijah, the Forerunner is also charged with turning "the hearts of fathers to their children… and to make ready a people prepared for the Lord" (Lk 1.17). There is urgency in establishing God's plan! One should level the paths, make strait what is crooked, that is, watch over the conditioning and the conversion of the human heart to permit the coming of the last and true Messiah, the third one after Elijah and John the Baptist, in the person of Jesus. This advent finds its anchor in human history, in

[1] Cf. Lk 6.45.

the changeover of the generations where the hearts of fathers and sons are called to be restored to one another, to beat in unison, to receive the ultimate revelation in order to harmonize the prophecies received by the fathers with the prophecies received by the sons. To make this harmony real is a delicate matter—the hearts of the fathers and sons very often remain separate.

Thus Scripture evokes what later was to be called (for example, in 1968) the conflict of generations; and this, in a biblical perspective, is opposed to the divine plan. Today it is still necessary to bring back the hearts of the fathers to their children, and children to fathers, so that they beat together in the expectation of "the great and dreadful day of the Lord."

Be like God

As he left the hands of his Creator, the human being was promised a life of perfect happiness, the only conceivable one in eternity. This was life in God. As descendants of the first man, we preserve, buried in the depths of our heart—in what Jung calls "the collective memory"—a longing, as it were, for this original happiness. This was at the dawn of the history of humankind, of this great Time before time, where everything was beautiful and full of joy. Sometimes we glimpse this felicity in the duration of lightning. It takes on the form of the transfigured face of the beloved being, of a sundown on a blue sea, set alight by rays, of a trill with which a bird sings about life. But such instants do not last. After inundating us with pleasure, they give way to the monotony of daily life, to the wearing down of things, to everything that on this earth arouses our sadness. Can one enjoy happiness when the latter does not last? The psalmist laments the brevity of man's life. It "flourishes like the flower of a field. For the wind passes over it, and it is gone.[2]" "O time, delay your flight! And you, happy times, delay your course," Lamartine replies as in an echo.

In paradise, man enjoyed a perfect happiness, being entirely immersed in the pure, divine light. He was unified, which is to say that all the components of his being—the mental, the heart, the powers of his spirit—lived in harmony in a state of an exceptional tension. His aim was to accomplish the tasks required by God: to grow and multiply, that is, to prolong and develop the divine creative act; to name all the living beings, that is to say, to have the power to distinguish between them (as one gives

---

[2] Ps 103[102].15–16.

a name to a new-born child), thereby possessing mastery over creation. He flourished at all points in the Creator's project, which was to become a partaker of his life of love.

St Macarius

The power of the soul which we call "intellect," what instruments does it use when it is active? No one has ever supposed that the intellect resided in the nails, in the eyebrows, in the nostrils, or the lips. Everybody agrees that it should be placed within us. But some have hesitated to define, inside the bowels, the organ which it uses in the first place. Indeed, some place the intellect in the brain, as in a type of acropolis; others speculate that its vehicle is the very center of the heart and what in the heart is from the animal breath. And we ourselves, we know from exact experience that our reason is neither inside us, as in a container, for it is incorporeal, nor in the outside, for it is attached to us, but that it is in the heart, as in its organ. We have received this not from man but from the Creator of man himself, who, in showing that "What goes into the mouth does not make a person unclean, but what comes out of his mouth" (Mt 15.11), says: "From the heart come evil thoughts" (Mt 15.19).

Now, love requires the gift of self, freely consented to. It does not allow the slightest constraint. God wants to deal only with beings that give themselves freely to him: "Henceforth I do not call you servants... but I have called you friends" (Jn 15.15), Jesus tells his disciples, reestablishing them in their original vocation of being "friends of God." Had man not had the possibility of turning away from this life of paradise, he would have been but a robot in the hands of the Almighty, a mechanism deprived of free will. The tree of the knowledge of good and evil stands in the middle of the garden, like a challenge God places before himself in order to put a limit to his almighty power and to give man the freedom of choice, without which there is no love. Man's freedom consists in being able to say, "No" to his Creator. Wanting to be free is to run the risk of suffering from it: "If you eat of it, you will die."[3] The challenge issued by God in planting the tree of the knowledge of good and evil was indeed

---

[3] Cf. Gn 2.17, 3.3.

the challenge of love, not the arbitrary act of a cruel, authoritarian God who takes pleasure in punishing his rebellious creature... The image of God without a heart, a sadist even for Freud, or even close to this admission made by Sartre in *The Words* [*Les Mots*]: "I expected a God; they offered me a Big Boss."

The day when man wanted to imitate, to "ape" God—"you will be like God," the serpent of Genesis said—he lost this life of happiness for which he had been created. The tragic consequence of the Fall is to submit man to time, and thus to old age with its procession of suffering and death. Man's inner being has been shattered. He has become broken down; his humor changes with every instant. He has become the prey of doubt, he resembles "a wave of the sea driven and tossed by the wind" (Jas 1.6), as James the Apostle writes. When Jesus comes near the Gerasene demoniac, he asks the demonic force: "What is your name?—Legion!"[4] The answer rings out and sends a shiver down the spine. "Legion" signifies we are a multitude—a Roman legion consisted of approximately 6,000 men—able to break, divide, and besiege an individual's inner being, make him lose his unity, demean him, force him into the worst follies.

Now, God will make an appearance upon the scene to lend a helping hand to the one he created through love. The entire history of the people of the first Covenant shows that God is seized by compassion before his creature's degeneration. Dominating the anger these men with stiff necks provoke in him, prompt as they are to adore idols, he lets his suffering be transparent before the misery of his people: "Even as a father has compassion upon his sons, so does the Lord have compassion upon those who fear him" (Ps 103.13[5]). He is moved by the trials that befall the nation he has chosen: "I have indeed seen the affliction of my people in Egypt, and I have heard their cry on account of their taskmasters; for I know their sufferings" (Ex 3.7). He then charges his servant Moses to free the people from servitude and lead them to the Promised Land. Thus, from the moment the fruit of the tree of knowledge is eaten, the heart of man loses its purity; tossed about by various movements, he avoids the control of reason, and a fatal schizophrenic dichotomy is created in him. This condition of the fallen heart, devoted to infinite torments, but always beating, is what moves the divine compassion: "The Spirit of the Lord... has sent me to bind up the broken-hearted" (Is 61.1).

[4]   Cf. Mk 5.9.

[5]   Ps 102.13 LXX.

This theme of the broken heart returns like a leitmotif in the Scriptures. When Jesus appears in the synagogue of Nazareth, he deliberately chooses this text from Isaiah to claim it for himself, to the astonishment of his audience: "Today this text has been fulfilled in your hearing" (Lk 4.21). At the moment he begins his missionary activity among the people, Jesus somehow announces its color, and exposes in what spirit he intends to act now. He has truly come to appease and console the broken-hearted. The serpent of Eden, God's adversary, suggested that man eat of the fruit in order "to be like God," so as to deprive him of his power and his strength, and rule in his stead. Jesus repeats the words of the serpent, though in a different manner. He too invites man to be "like God," not to enter into a desire of rivalry, but to open the pathways of mercy and allow the human heart to expand into infinity. To become sovereign through love, not force...

God Probes the Hearts

God is a "raging fire" from which his creature flees for fear of being burned. A vain effort! The one who turns his heart away from the Lord is damned. Since Cain, we know that no one can shy away from the gaze of the heavenly judge who pursues the criminal with his justice, beyond the grave. The famous verse of Victor Hugo says, "The eye was in the tomb and looked at Cain." God "knows the hidden things of the heart" (Ps 44.21[6]). In his perception, "God probes the hearts and reins" (Ps 7.9[7]), these hidden zones, buried in the substructures—in the subconscious, one would say today—where the powers of desire swarm, and violent passions flare up, the contradictory impulses that elude the power of the rational "me." Nothing escapes God's vigilance. He is the great psychoanalyst, able to probe "the reins and the hearts," to "bring to light their maneuvers."[8] Such is the scriptural vision of man dissociated, divided among the various components of his being that wage a war without mercy. God "weighs the hearts"[9] is another way of saying that he reveals their vanity or their duplicity. He is more intimate to the heart of man than man himself can be to what is most intimate to him. Nothing of

---

[6] Ps 43.22 LXX.

[7] In some versions, 7.10. Cf. Rev 2.23.—Ed.

[8] Cf. Jer 11.18.

[9] Prov 21.2; 24.2.

what boils in the heart escapes a God who "probes the hearts." Ultimately, the last word belongs to him, "For nothing is hidden but it will be made clear, nothing secret but it will be made known."[10]

It is appropriate to delineate clearly the domain that depends on psychoanalysis, on the observation of the sources of the psychic life, from the domain that depends on the life of the Spirit and his own laws. The two domains, one of which is the fruit of human knowledge, and the other of divine power and grace, can have numerous points of contact without being confused one for the other. Long before Freud and modern psychoanalysis, the Apostle Paul was conscious of being inhabited by a force that contradicted his will. He calls this force "sin": "I do not do what I want to do.... And if I do what I do not want to do, it is no more that I that do it, but sin that dwells in me" (Rm 7.15–17). This unfortunate condition of human life forces Pascal to exclaim: "How hollow and foul is the heart of man!" Borrowing an image from the prophet Jeremiah, he views the heart as a "cistern."[11] Its bottom is a cesspit, full of sludge, blocked by strange vegetation, poisonous plants that bring death. Leaning over the edge of this cistern, Pascal casts on it looks of horror, and he pulls back while shaking: "I see my abyss of pride, of curiosity, of concupiscence... This infinite abyss cannot be filled except by God himself." In his heart, he touches the depths of dereliction, and he turns away from this spectacle that fills him with disgust: "The 'me' is hateful," he says.

It would be good to give future priests a solid foundation in psychology so that they do not too quickly call "sin" what comes under the jurisdiction of a neurosis. For their part, the psychoanalysts should know, as some do, that alongside the analytical discourse there are other means that have proven their worth, such as the granting of forgiveness by the heavenly Father, love given and received, brotherly sharing, to bind up the wounds of bruised hearts, leading them out of their frozen loneliness, and giving a new meaning to their existence.

The true and the false, sincerity and appearance, confront one another in the moving condition of fallen man whom Isaiah the prophet denounces: "This people draw near me with their mouth, and with their lips they honor me, but they have removed their hearts far from me" (Is 29:13). In this colorful style proper to the Semites, the idea of the heart "removed from God" portrays, with a note of desolation, this

---

[10]   Mt 10.6; Lk 12.2.

[11]   Jer 2.13, cf. Isaiah 36.16.

state of indifference with respect to the divine. It points to this dramatic lack of interest in the meaning of life that has strangely spread in this post-industrial consumer society, in which man may believe himself to be self-satisfied. There he is, eating once more, and greedily, the fruit of the tree of knowledge. "You will be like gods," today means, "You can do without God." "God? I never think of him," Françoise Sagan said a short time ago,[12] and the statement connoted, in spite of everything, that he possibly might exist. It is a question not only of asking what man thinks of God, but of what God thinks of man.

What is at stake is considerable. In terms of oppositions, it appears as paradoxical as may be the warm and the cold in the subtitle of the acts of a colloquy held at Paray-le-Monial on October 13–15, 1999, *Pour une civilisation du coeur* [For a Civilization of the Heart, Toward a Freezing or a Warming of the World?][13] For the members of this colloquy, the people of our time have allowed the requirements of the heart to atrophy. A silent restlessness weighs upon today's world. Its state of certain places is eloquent by itself. The desire to consume—however necessary this might be for the planet's underprivileged—the rush to unbridled pleasure, the multiplication of television programs or of information on the Internet often prove to be a flight from reality. The rift between the well-to-do and those who live below the poverty level, the terrible threat that fanatics equipped with destructive forces inflict (among which is the atomic peril), the corruption in business circles, the ascendancy of hatred in unending conflicts are only a few of the constants. Heartless men? It is urgent to recommend a return to the deep sources the heart conceals, a heart from which life pours out, a heart in search of a hearing.

The multiplication of psychoanalysis offices and of psychological therapies are a sign of the disarray of the human being confronted by the evil of living. The latter reveals the discrepancy between a technology that is more and more refined, and a human psyche threatened by a breaking point. Father Alexander Men, the Russian priest assassinated in 1990 for having been a witness to the Good News, maintained straightforwardly that the one who would practice even half of the Beatitudes would be freed from all his neuroses. "Blessed are the pure in heart, for they shall see God" (Mt 5.8), Jesus announces. Purity of heart: there is one of the answers to the morbid affections of the modern world.

[12] This work was originally published in 2004, the same year in which Françoise Sagan died.—Ed.

[13] *Pour une civilisation du cœur* (Paris: Éditions de l'Emmanuel, 2000).

Feeling and Thinking with the Heart

Scriptural anthropology is "heart-centered," which is to say, that the heart is the central focus of the person, "the focus of the soul," according to the nineteenth-century Russian thinker, Ivan Kireyevsky. It opens an inward space where the powers of life are born. In the first rank of the latter are the feelings, then emotions capable of disturbing its rhythm, desires, the will, the decisive choices as conceived easily by the amateur common sense of the press of the heart. As a prey to strong agitations, the heart is frequently associated with the entrails. The image of the entrails designates this elementary, primordial foundation, of the psychic life from which may well up the emotions that contribute to the advent of life through love and compassion, or conversely, of its disintegration through hatred and cruelty. "Behold, O Lord, for I am in distress: my bowels are troubled, mine heart is turned within me" (Lam 1.20).

Sometimes the current passes between man and God. The feelings are transmitted from heart to heart: "My son, if your heart is wise, then you will gladden my heart also" (Prov 23.15). Man is a poor judge of the struggle between good and evil that is waged in his depths; he is afraid of not being able to love in truth, as St John says, but "If our heart condemns us, God is greater than our heart, and he knows all things" (1 Jn 3.20). Thus, the heart is the place where the powers of the psychic life are worked out, if one admits that it symbolizes the point where the conscious and the unconscious energies of being meet. It is there that the energies of the affective life coexist more or less peacefully, and also, no matter how surprising this may seem, those of the intellectual life and of the spiritual life, as Semitic thought has interpreted them... The psychology of the Semites, one may say, is of a materialistic character; it designates the facts of the psychic life with the name of the organ that concerns them, or by the effect they produce on this organ; and the latter is mainly the heart, which thereby happens to be at the same time the seat of the emotions, the feelings, intelligence and thought, and the moral and religious life."[14]

The faculty of thinking the Scriptures attribute to the heart is indeed rather unexpected. By making man in his image, the Creator has given him a tongue to speak, eyes to see, ears to hear and, to crown everything, a heart to reflect and not only to love. The words of God "judge the

---

[14] A. Guillaumont, "Les sens des noms du cœur dans l'Antiquité," in *Le Cœur*, op. cit., p. 51.

intents and the thoughts of the heart."[15] The highest meditations mature in the heart where "God has placed the thought of eternity" (cf. Eccl 3.11), and where he has written his laws (cf. Rom 2.15). The smallest nooks of the human heart could therefore not escape the knowledge of God, whose words "judge the intents and the thoughts of the heart." To say of an insane person that he has "no heart" is the same as saying that he does not have the ability to reason. The request, "My son, give me your heart," is devoid of affective connotations and signifies, "My son, pay attention to me."

The man who is thinking is said to speak to his heart, as with someone else, according to a curious process of doubling: "Abraham... spoke in his heart, saying: is a child to be born to a man one hundred years old?"[16] Every being that thinks takes himself as an interlocutor. Thus, the rich man says to his soul, "My soul... rest... rejoice."[17] The prodigal son, as a result of his debauched life where he squandered his share of the fortune, becomes poor like Job; at the moment of making a crucial decision, "...he came to his senses and said: ...I will go to my father and say..." (Lk 15.17–29). To think is therefore to take counsel with oneself, to meditate in one's heart that is then taken as a confidant, and that demarcates the space of interiority of being where the great options are worked out.

The heart is also the seat of memory. Does one not say in English, "learning by heart"? Man is invited to engrave the Lord's commandments in the heart: "And these words, all that I command you this day, shall be in your hearts" (Dt 6:6). Or God even undertakes to do it himself: "I will surely put my laws into their mind, and write them in their hearts" (Jer 31.33). The law is not reduced to a code of abstract principles. It signifies infinitely more. It is a word dictated by God. It is even possible to say that God is present in his Law, hence the religious veneration with which it was surrounded. If the law is engraved in the heart, it is there that God finds a place of predilection, a place of remembrance, a place of communion. St Paul writes to the Corinthians, "[You are] a Letter from Christ, written... with the Spirit of the living God, not on tablets of stone, but on tablets of hearts of flesh" (2 Cor 3.3). As a good Pharisee, the Apostle knows the metaphors of the Old Testament and he lets them spin to work out a vision of the new man inhabited by the Word.

---

[15] Hb 4.12.

[16] Gen 17.17.

[17] Cf. Lk 12.19.

The Israelites did not know that the brain, the existence of which was unknown to them, plays a crucial role in the development of thought. And yet they were not wrong in believing in a very strong bond between the activity of the mental and the affective power enclosed in the heart. Located in the very center of the human being, at the junction of the inner movements that weave the tissue of life, is the heart not in constant interaction with the brain? Lodged at an extremity, the latter can either sever itself from this source of vital energy, or drink from it in order to give shape to his thoughts... A thought that is proud of its rationality but cut off from the living sources welling up in the heart, does it not lead to a shriveling of being? With concern, God leans towards this place of integration of the human forces, "Within them I shall plant my Law, writing it in their hearts" (Jer 31.33[18]). The covenant with God, written in indelible ink, can be enacted in one's innermost being, a covenant which has at its base human thought, turned towards his Creator.

Knowing God in One's Heart

The heart is this central point where God and the human being meet one another and start a dialogue. God gives the people a clean heart so that they know he is their Lord. He reveals to them his own heart, so that they learn his intentions from age to age. Between them a heart-to-heart dialogue is formed, "A man's heart devises his way. The Lord directs his steps."[19] The heart, which is also the seat of the will, pushes man to act, to adopt this or that manner of conduct. It is an arena where a permanent fight takes place between the antagonistic forces that push man hither and yon. When the people follow "the inclinations of their evil heart,"[20] instead of searching for God with all their heart and confiding in him, they fall under the influence of an indocile and rebellious heart, a divided heart. Untold miseries then befall them. If man repents, one says that "he returns to his heart," following the example of David who, his crime committed, returns to repentance with "a broken spirit."[21] When man does not repent, he closes his heart, and "hardens it."

In a striking oracle of Ezekiel, man is invited to bring his heart into

---

[18] Jer 38.33 LXX.

[19] Prov 16.19.

[20] Jer 3.17, 7.24, 11.8, 13.10.

[21] Cf. Ps 51.17 [Ps 50.19 LXX].

compliance with the demands of the divine heart by the power of the Spirit: "I shall sprinkle clean water over you and you will be cleansed of all your uncleanness and all your idols. I shall give you a new heart, and put a new spirit in you. I shall remove the heart of stone from your flesh and I shall give you a heart of flesh instead. I shall put my spirit in you, and cause you to walk in my ordinances and to keep my judgments, and do them" (Ezek 36.25-27). In these words of the prophet, the heart is the matrix where the new life originates. It is a life to which God calls people, a life in which one moves from the age of stone to the age of flesh. Stone evokes hardness, a gravity that pulls downward, closure. Under the effect of grace that lightens, the flesh opens, elevates, evokes the one who is "meek and humble of heart,"[22] unfailingly attentive to the heart that beats in everyone's breast.

---

[22] Cf. Mt 11.29.

3

The Prayer of the Heart

Praying with One's Heart

Praying can be done in many ways. The first school of prayer is the liturgical office, in church, where all the members of the assembly, from children to older people, are united in common prayer. The beauty, the depth of the mystery of the "service of the people"—such is the meaning of the word liturgy—before God depends on the fervor each one brings to it. Before going to church, one prepares oneself for the encounter with a God full of light, as for an encounter with one's brothers, one should "dress up the heart," as the fox of the *Little Prince* would say before sitting down at the banquet of love.

Prayer can also be done by repeating prayers with fixed formulations proposed by the Church in manuals of prayer. The prayers mark the different moments of the day: one does not pray in the evening in the same spirit as in the morning. They also marks the different seasons of the year: the tonality of prayer in the Christmas season is not the same as during Pascha time. One prays to express a request or to give thanks, on the occasion of a trip, an illness, an examination, a bereavement, when one repents... In all these cases the Church lends her support by proposing words for one to address to God, words to which one is asked to adjust the movements of one's heart. Orthodox prayer books generally open with the following advice: "After waiting for a moment during which all your emotions quiet down and all your thoughts leave behind all earthly preoccupation, pronounce the words of the prayer, without haste, by making your heart pay attention."

Sometimes, the words that arise from the depth of the heart pour out freely in a spontaneous beseeching or praise. A mother whose child is gravely ill will find enough words to cry out her despair. Before the beauty of the world one will glorify God in the visible creation, as St Paul invites him to it. Marveling at the splendor of nature, the Romantic poet Keats cries out, "A thing of beauty is a joy for ever."

Some embark on the practice of the "prayer of the heart," generally called the "Jesus Prayer." It would be more exact to say the "Prayer to Jesus." It is indeed to him that the prayer is addressed. It is toward the person of the Savior that the one who asks of him his grace, his presence, turns himself. Here is the typical form, the one used most frequently: "Lord Jesus Christ, Son of God, have mercy on me, a sinner." No one should devote oneself to the practice of this repetitive prayer without having received beforehand an imperative appeal from the Lord and, if possible, having this verified by a competent confessor. The "mechanical" aspect of this type of prayer outside of its ecclesial and sacramental content, can be a source of illusion.

Father Sophrony

The place of prayer and of the spiritual life, because it is also the core of being where its unity is achieved, is the heart. The Lord's appeal is addressed above all to the heart as the person's spiritual center. The love of God is born in the heart through faith, and then the flame of this love attracts the intellect to it; having become like melting wax, the intellect is then joined to the heart and contemplates Being in the light of divine love.

In the East, the Desert Fathers established this tradition of prayer called "prayer of the heart" or "Jesus Prayer," since the name of the Savior, bearer of his presence, resonates at its center. The heart is the luminous center of it. This prayer has spread to a number of Catholic as well as Protestant circles as, for example, the Protestant movement of the "Watchmen," which centers the life of the Christian in contemplative prayer. I am sometimes asked to share with Christian brothers my rather poor experience in this domain, which hardly reaches beyond the first mumblings. At the close of an ecumenical gathering in the region of Poitiers, the inviting Catholic priest had recommended to the participants to return home while quietly and humbly reciting this prayer, since the presentation of it had struck them. The prayer of the heart had created a strong moment of communion among them.

In nineteenth-century Russia a little book appeared, *The Pilgrim's*

Tale, whose hero travels on all the roads of the country while carefully guarding in his heart this prayer centered on the name of Jesus. The man tells how this habit of mystical wandering was born in him. When he had lost his wife and all his possessions in a fire, he entered a church one day and heard these words: "Pray without ceasing" (1 Thess 5.17), which engraved themselves in his mind in fiery letters. How is it possible to pray uninterruptedly? He was to know no peace until he had obtained an answer, for he felt an urgent call to put this exhortation into practice. After moving heaven and earth in the search for someone able to teach him how to maintain in himself a permanent state of prayer, he ended up finding a *staretz*, that is to say, a monk gifted with discernment, who transmitted to him the heritage of this prayer, which is more precisely transmission of a lived experience, from person to person, to allow beginners to avoid false steps into illusion. The brevity and the repetitive character of the formula allow one to restrain the perpetual wandering ways of the mind, with the result that one is led to a condition of calmness, perseverance, and courage, in the assurance of going toward a personal God. The staretz teaches the pilgrim how "to let the intellect descend into the heart," that is to say, how to unify the states of prayer, to center and integrate them in the "deep me." There the latter discovers the One who is love and can become a bearer of this ineffable love in the world that surrounds him, for without love the prayer is sterile. Strengthened with this *viaticum*, the mystic vagabond then sets off into the vast spaces of the Russian plain, living in intimacy with his Lord. Like the apostle of the gentiles, he can then cry out: "I live, yet not I, but Christ lives in me."[1]

The prayer must be maintained with perseverance against wind and tide, as the apostle says, "We do not know what we should ask."[2] Only the frequency has been left to our power as a means to obtain the purity that is the mother of any spiritual good. The quality does not depend on us, but we can offer to God the quantity by rendering it as transparent as is in our power. Here is how it is recommended to the pilgrim to deepen his experience: "When someone offends me, I remember how sweet the Jesus prayer is and the offense and anger disappear and I forget everything. I walk in a semiconscious state without worries, interests, or temptations. My only desire and attraction is for solitude and ceaseless recitation of the Jesus prayer. This makes me happy. God knows what this is all about.

[1] Gal 2.20.
[2] Cf. Rom 8.26.

Certainly, all this is on the sensuous level, or, as the late elder said, it is a natural and artificial result of habit. I am not yet ready to make the interior prayer of the heart my own…"[3]

On many occasions Scripture describes the continuity of the state of prayer: "Lord, God of my salvation, I cry before you day and night."[4] Or also, "I sleep but my heart is awake."[5] Certain Gospel figures do not cease harassing the Lord with their supplications: the two blind men on the road to Jericho: "Lord, Son of David, have mercy on us!";[6] the Canaanite woman whose daughter is dying: "Lord, Son of David, have mercy on me!";[7] the publican: "O God, have mercy on me, a sinner!"[8] The Lord approves of the widow who presses the unjust judge with her importunity until she wins her case. For all of them it is a question of life or death… Such is indeed the state of mind in which each ought to say daily prayers as if his own life depended on them. The focused prayer of all these men and women bears salvation, because it is heard each time. In the garden of Gethsemane, "…after visiting his disciples for a third time," Christ himself prayed "by repeating the same words."[9]

It is not indispensable to vary the register of words or ideas. It suffices that they carry the one thing necessary. The formulation of the Jesus prayer becomes crystallized among the Desert Fathers, beginning in the fourth century.

The prayer has a profoundly evangelical basis to the degree it is centered on the person of the Savior and it repeats, at least in part, the words of the blind men, of the Canaanite woman, the publican, caught in an uninterrupted state. In Scripture, the one who is invoked is present in his name. This is the reason why the Hebrews did not pronounce the name of *Yahweh*—the Greek equivalent of which is *Kyrie*, the pre-eminently divine name—except for the High Priest, once year, on the day of Yom Kippur. Indeed, by virtue of the transcendence with which it was

---

[3] *The Way of a Pilgrim* and *The Pilgrim Continues His Way*, trans. by Helen Bacovcin (Garden City, NY: Image Books, 1978), p. 24.

[4] Cf. Ps 87.2 LXX [88.1 KJV].

[5] Song 5.2.

[6] Mt 20.30–31, cf. 9.27.

[7] Mt 15.22.

[8] Lk 18.13.

[9] Cf. Mt 26.44.

invested, this name instilled in them a feeling of mystic fear. The Jews have inculcated the correct attitude before the awesomeness of the Most High. With the incarnation, this transcendence is not abolished; it is surpassed by the lowering of the Son of Man under the traits of the suffering servant who is in charge of human nature. Now Jesus himself communicates his presence by giving men the gift of his name: "If you ask for anything in my name, I will do it" (Jn 14.14).The ancestral fear is banished, a serene and loving communion with the divine can be established with all people. Invoking the name of the Lord is to let it descend into the depths of one's heart.

Father Sophrony

Eternity entered sweetly but forcefully into my heart, and my mind knew the blessedness of feeling oneself melting in the flame of love coming from the heart. This fusion of my entire being, of the mind, the heart, and the body, gave me a feeling of the integrity of being, a state as different as possible from the habitual division of mind, soul, and body.

The prayer to Jesus answers a double exigency. The first, as St Paul expresses it, consists in turning to Jesus for the great occasions as well as small occupations of daily life: "And whatever you say or do, do all in the name of the Lord Jesus" (Col 3.17). Its concision banishes the dispersion of the attention, eliminates any intellectual effort, and continually reduces the movie of the inner life to what is essential: the presence of the Lord who is "meek and humble of heart."[10] The mind is immersed in God, be it only for a brief instant. One word or another may be trimmed from the formula, until it is sometimes reduced to the mere repetition of the name of Jesus that contains all. Its designation under the name "prayer to Jesus" indicates that it is centered entirely on the name of the Lord, who represents its radiant heart, its peace-bringing presence, and the appeal to union with him. In *The Pilgrim's Tale*, someone asks the question: how can one recite the prayer when one has to accomplish a task that requires the entire concentration of one's mental energies? By way of an answer, it is proposed that one imagine an architect whom a king orders to draw up the plans of his palace. He will have to work

---

[10] Mt 11.29.

on the steps of the throne, in the august presence, the aura, the aura of his king. If one cannot pronounce the words, one can always arouse the presence by an initial invocation and achieve one's task by the radiance of this presence. A father driving his family in a car will not bury himself in prayers that run the risk of distracting his attention, but he can act with a feeling of Christ's presence, which will help him perhaps in pushing back any upsurge of impatience or anger in case of difficulty.

The second exigency consists of establishing one's heart, one's innermost "me" in calmness and in letting the prayer follow its course peacefully toward the One who gives peace, and not "as the world gives it."[11] Entering into the peace of Christ is to unite oneself to a person, with the One who reveals a peace coming from elsewhere. From this exigency there developed a great spiritual movement called "hesychasm" which, in Greek, signifies calmness, peace. Born in the desert of the Thebaïd in the third century, this movement later spread to central Europe and Russia, and it is now found all over the entire modern world where one can find monks and lay people who practice this form of prayer, for example, in Paris, London, or New York. This latter city was chosen by the American novelist J. D. Salinger, in *Franny and Zooey*, as a theater of discussion around the Jesus Prayer between a rather skeptical brother and his sister, who practices the prayer, two young intellectuals "connected" to New York society.

Modern man has an extra-sensitive nervous system; he is not very resistant to the trials of existence. The emotions, the worries, the anxiety of living in a world where God is absent and where one has made a clean sweep (*tabula rasa*) of the hope of the Gospel, has put his psychic nature to a severe test. They overwhelm him with fatigue, compel him to multiply the psychological aids trying to cure it. The prayer of the heart is not just one more psychological aid or therapeutic supplement to be used when classical therapy is insufficient. It recalls for man the norm of his nature which is to be a child of the love of God, invited to let this love radiate around him. If God wants it, the prayer, by fixing itself on the one who is the Prince of Peace, unifies the disordered strivings of the psyche, purifies the impure feelings, dissipates the stained images, the corrosive ideas that are a source of fatigue. It is this way whether one lives in a hermitage in the deep desert or one paces up and down on the arteries swarming with people of a large modern city. The biographer of

[11] Jn 24.27.

St Honoratus, founder of the monastery at Lérins, writes that he prayed much, that he was always joyful. Then he adds this unexpected detail: that gave him peaceful sleep! It is always possible to see the person of Christ on the tired faces, faces sometimes closed, that one encounters on the metro, in the supermarket, faces that a spark of hope would make joyful. The peace of the one who, by grace, has overcome the division of his being can be contagious: "Acquire inner peace and crowds of people will be saved," St Seraphim of Sarov said.

Entering into the Heart

Western thought is an analytical thought that loves to decompose the elements submitted to its reflection. Semitic thought is a synthetic, unifying thought that aims at recapturing the totality of being. Ignoring Platonic philosophy's dualist distinction between the soul and the body, the tradition of the Christian East remains related to the Semitic tradition where the heart is the constituent element and the human being's center of integration. All activity is founded on it. All movements of the spiritual life are born from it and end in it. It is the place where the Holy Spirit and the devil confront one another, as Dostoevsky writes in *The Brothers Karamazov*, when Dimitri, the oldest one, exclaims before his younger brother Alyosha: "Do you know this mystery? It is the duel between the devil and God, and the human heart is the battle ground." It is in the heart that the human being decides his destiny.

Between the heart, open to all natural and supernatural realities and the head, the seat of the intellectual faculties, a fatal dissociation has appeared, a consequence of the Fall. The prayer of the heart comes to repair this ontological wound in an effort to reunite these two components of the human being, all too frequently dissociated, in a harmonious state conquered in a noble struggle. "When the intellect and the heart are united in prayer... the heart is warmed in a spiritual warmth, and the light of Christ shines in it, filling the inner man with peace and joy," Seraphim of Sarov writes. With years, through an effort of imitation, the faces of certain Mount Athos monks end up resembling those of the saints painted on the frescoes along the corridors of their monasteries, where they walk back and forth, day and night, to go to their services. Through an invocation repeated endless times, a human being ends up resembling the object of his prayer. He transforms himself into the object of his love.

The masters of the spiritual life highlight the opposition between external and internal prayer. Be it said vocally or mentally, but without the participation of the "deep me," prayer remains external. Interiorizing prayer is within everybody's reach, on condition of entering into the heart: "But you, when you pray, go into your room, close the door, and pray to your Father who is there in secret" (Mt 6.6). This secret room represents both the concrete place where man retires to say his prayers and the symbolic place of the heart where he goes to the Father who secretly waits for his arrival. It constitutes this inner cell where, according to St Macarius, are contained "all the passions and all the vices, but also God, the angels and the Kingdom, light, the apostles, and the treasures of grace." Jesus also proposes that the Kingdom of God is inside man or in the midst of people. The Gospel has the highest understanding possible about the spiritual riches that man carries within, hidden from external view. "When we are in the heart, we are at home, when we are not there, we are homeless," Theophan the Recluse adds. When he exiles himself from his heart, a human being becomes a person without a fixed abode in the world of the Spirit. But unlike his homeless brother one sees wandering in the great city, he carries in his heart an inalienable possibility of relocation. He can always reintegrate his inner dwelling.

Descending into the Arena of the Heart

God and Satan are engaged in combat in the arena of the heart, as the entire work of Dostoevsky and of so many other novelists try to demonstrate. In order to come out the winner in the trials and tribulations, one should find a spiritual guide, a sure judge, like the staretz Zosima toward Alyosha Karamazov. Can this guide not be found? God will provide for this, say the masters of the spiritual life. He does not leave man abandoned. Each should understand the meaning of his condition, purify his inner being in suffering and in the tears of repentance. Metropolitan Innocent of Moscow maintains that, when the Holy Spirit enters into the heart of man, he "reveals to him all the sins that coexist in him." Then man can perform an act of contrition and pass through the fire of humility.

Great vigilance is required to discern the movements of the heart. "After each thought has been chased away from the soul by the remembrance of the presence of God, one should stand at the door of one's heart and keep attentive watch over everything that enters and leaves from there," Theophan the Recluse comments. This vigilance, this fixing of the attention in the heart, imposes itself on all occasions of daily life to cut short the surges of anger, the loss of composure, easy judgments, impure desires; they should be uprooted the moment they are born. When Christ says that "anyone who looks at a woman to lust for her has already committed adultery with her in his heart" (Mt 5.28), he knows well that the sight of a woman can give birth to an involuntary desire. It is all a question of knowing whether man eradicates it on the spot or entertains it with complacency. Indeed, he then commits "adultery in the heart" which is already condemned in a manner of a progression to the deed.

If a thought troubles the spirit by awakening evil desires in it, it is possible to fight this by opposing to it a contrary thought and imploring the pardon of God so that it is substituted for the first one. Thus, to avarice is opposed the desire to give alms, to gluttony, abstinence from food. The vigilance exercised on the movement of the heart does not have to imprison man in himself in a continual tension. One should also open one's prayers on the world, on the people who surround us, especially those whose body and soul are wounded; one should feel the palpitation of life. Who knows, the spiritual men say, if such a prayer will not go to the end of the world and prevent someone from drowning in despair? In whatever place it might be, in the street or in the subway, it is always possible through prayer to act so that earth and heaven meet in the heart of the one who elevates his thought to God. This heart offers to him all those who, around him, attend to their business. The name of Jesus is seen on their face. Then will it perhaps be given to discern in their features the face of Christ: "After God, see God in every human being" the patristic saying has it.

"Know thyself" (*gnothi seauton*): such was the motto of Socrates. The spiritual Fathers go back to this philosophic step, because for them, "as long as the soul is not established with the intellect in the heart, she does not see herself and is truly not aware of herself. Knowing oneself is indispensable in order not be tempted to criticize others: the one who works to know himself does not have time to notice the faults of others. Judge yourselves and you will cease judging others. Consider every human being as being better than you are," Theophan the Recluse adds. Certain spiritual men even say that true love consists not only in loving one's neighbor as oneself but even more than oneself. Indeed, the ultimate contests are being fought in the arena of the heart.

Persevering in the Place of the Heart

"Pray always, in the Spirit, with prayer and supplications" St Paul writes.[12] Far from being an activity limited to precise moments—like Liturgy on a Sunday morning—prayer is a permanent state of the mind. The state of the betrothed of the Song of Songs who expects the return of her beloved and never ceases thinking of him... How much more attractive the external activities of man appear to man than the activity of prayer with its sobriety, its aridity! The appeal of inwardness is interrupted by the fascination with images and the voices of this world. One must descend again and again into one's own depths to rekindle the spirit of zeal. Repeated with perseverance, this exercise prevents the soul from growing dumb. In an apophthegm of the Desert Fathers, an old monk was at the point of dying. When he came near his bed, one of the brothers who kept him company at the end of his life did not ask the question usually asked: "How are you feeling?" He asked, "How is your prayer life? Are you really maintaining it?" Thus supported, the dying brother was able to keep his mind lucid until his last breath. Likewise, it is said of the early Christians that, when they met one another, they exchanged not a banal "How are you?" but "How is your prayer life?" Certain spiritual men advise that one should give oneself to prayer as if it were the first time, to renew the enthusiasm and the fervor one has at the beginning of a new activity. One of them warns earnestly: "If you do not succeed in prayer, do not hope to succeed with other things. For prayer is the root of all."

The uninterrupted state of his prayer is described by the Russian pilgrim as follows: "I acquired the habit of the prayer of the heart so well that I practiced it unceasingly and, in the end, I sensed that it said it itself, without any activity on my part; it welled up from my mind and in my heart. Not only in a state of being awake but also during sleep, and it was not interrupted for one second." Indeed the human being can find himself in two contrasting states of prayer. Sometimes it is the fruit of a conscious activity of man depending upon the will, sometimes it is given to man by grace, independently of his efforts. A woman was gravely ill, and her spiritual father encouraged her to persevere in prayer by devoting all her strength to it. But her strength declined. Shortly before dying she wrote to him: "I am exhausted, and when I no longer have the strength to pray, I feel that Christ picks up the baton; it is he who prays in my place." It is not possible to elevate oneself to such a prayer on the strength of

---

[12] Eph 6.18.

one's desire, for it is given by grace, and moved by the Spirit; it is given only to those whose heart has been purified. It is no longer the human being who prays by imploring the Spirit; it is the Spirit who prays in him.

The Heart and the Sacramental Union with God

"Lord Jesus Christ, Son of God, have mercy on me, a sinner!" The prayer of the heart rests on a dogmatic foundation that is perfectly accurate. At the opening, the one to whom one turns is the Lord (*Kyrios*). The Lord Jesus Christ is designated by the personal name, Jesus, which was given to him by his mother, as well as by the name of the One whom Israel expected, the Christ, that is, the Anointed, the Messiah sent by God. His relationship with the Father is indicated well, in such a way that this prayer, centered on the name of Jesus, introduces one into the intimacy of the Trinity. The Holy Spirit is equally present, if only in the act of invocation. Indeed, as St Paul states, "No one can say 'Jesus is Lord!' except by the Holy Spirit" (1 Cor 12.3). The Holy Spirit comes to one's aid to pronounce the name of the Lord and to manifest his presence in the heart of man. The attitude of the latter in the face of the divine is specified: he is a sinner, expecting or hoping for pity and forgiveness. As a matter of fact, the translation of the Greek word *eleison* with "have pity" or "take pity" does not present the semantic richness of this verb. Through the stem *el-aion*, which signifies oil, it evokes anointing, grace.[13] Indeed, a translation that would be closer to the *Kyrie eleison* could be, "Have mercy on me and cover me with your grace." The Russian term *pomilui* corresponds better to it as does the English expression "have mercy."

In order to embark on this prayer, one should have heard a call. One should equally cultivate in oneself a feeling of deep repentance by becoming aware of one's sinful state, without which the *eleison* would no longer have any meaning. The repentance in question is not a banal regret for having acted badly or for having given in to sin. It evokes something that is much more important, which is a true turnabout of the deep heart. It is related to the firm and definitive decision to change one's conduct, to lead one's life not in conformity with the laws of this world, but in obedience to the commandments of Christ, "A new commandment I give you: love one another, as I have loved you" (Jn 13.34). The most characteristic example is that of the Prodigal Son. After squandering his part of the fortune in wild living, and being reduced to misery, he "came to himself,

---

[13] Not all scholars agree on this etymological connection.—Ed.

and said..." The expression "came to himself" is the equivalent of "he recovered the path to his heart." It is then that he decided to return to his father and to radically change his way of life. Such is repentance in its most demanding form.

During the unfolding of the liturgical service, the deacon asks for attention in the heart of the faithful, "Let us say with all our soul and with all our mind, let us say..." The assembly responds *Kyrie eleison*— that is, "Lord, have mercy, and cover us with your grace." According to historians, this *Kyrie eleison* repeated ceaselessly represents the original core of the prayer of supplication. In early times, the assembly gathered around the *Kyrie*, the name of Lord, the bearer of his presence, and then organically the requests pour out, and, like powerful waves, they put at the feet of the Lord the needs, the sufferings, the acts of thanksgiving of his people. The overflowing of the heart can thus be poured out freely before the one who is "good and a friend of man."

As the place of encounter between God and man, the heart of the believer symbolizes this innermost being where the substance of the sacraments is placed to make new life well up from it. As the pastor Jacques Serr notes, "The Jesus Prayer can dwell only in the baptized heart. It is baptism that regenerates the heart in the name of the Father, of the Son, and of the Holy Spirit." He adds, "Baptism by aspersion touches only the front and the head, while by immersion, the entire body, and thus the heart, is plunged into the water of regeneration."

For its part, the Eucharist equally transmits to the entire body the fire of the divine energy. This is indicated with a profound realism in the thanksgiving prayer of Symeon Metaphrastes: "You who are a fire consuming the unworthy, consume me not, O my Creator, but instead enter into my members, my veins, my heart."

Sown in the heart of man, the Jesus Prayer rejoins the prayer of the Church, where her deep heart beats to the rhythm of the liturgies. By ever widening concentric circles, it rejoins the heart of the world and of nature, called to transfiguration. The Russian pilgrim describes this mystery as follows: "The prayer of the heart consoled me to such a degree that I considered myself the happiest man on earth and I wondered whether the beatific vision could bring any greater consolation. I am so happy that I did not think one could be happier on earth... This happiness illumined not only my inner soul; the world outside also appeared to me in a ravishing light; everything called me to love and praise God: people, the trees, the plants, the animals, everything was familiar to me and everywhere I found the image of the name Jesus Christ. Sometimes I felt so light that I believed I no longer had a body… Sometimes I entered entirely in myself. I clearly saw my interior, and I admired the admirable edifice of the human body."[14] Such were the ecstatic feelings with which the Russian pilgrim was overwhelmed when he made his way in nature. When one thinks of the phenomenon of ecstasy, one imagines rather a man sitting or standing, frozen in an almost quasi-absolute immobility. The immobility is a sign that any bodily or psychic agitation has been quieted. But here, the mystic vagabond moves. The movement does not prevent him from experiencing this ineffable feeling of being projected out of his body. Concretely, he joins the cosmic song uttered by all living creatures according to the psalmist's injunction, "Let every breath praise the Lord" (Ps 150.6).

Union with the Savior can lead to the state in which, thanks to the persevering prayer of the name of Jesus, "the heart absorbs the Lord and the Lord absorbs the heart," as St John Chrysostom puts it magnificently. In this vital union, where it is given to man to live in God with the intellect and in the heart, he accomplishes the aim of his life. He achieves the end for which he has been created. Theophan the Recluse adds: "Those who seek this vital union should not be troubled if they do not achieve important things in the external domain. This work contains in itself all the other activities."

---

[14] Op. cit., p. 85.

4

THE HEART AT PEACE: HESYCHASM

Opening one's heart also means to have the heart at peace in the encounter with the other and the Entirely-Other. All Christian traditions have much to say about this theme, and they can only enrich one another. The specific contribution of the Christian East derives from a deep current of spirituality: hesychasm. It is proper to the East, but it spreads easily to the western sphere of Christianity where it keeps attracting a good number of minds in search of a method or an experience of the spiritual life. The word hesychasm (pronounce the "ch" like a "k"), or *hesychia* in Greek, signifies rest, calmness, peace, and silence. It is a state of life, or rather, a wisdom of life, where action or asceticism alternates with contemplation. At the source of hesychasm is a collection of texts: the *Philokalia*.

The Philokalia

Philokalia means "love of the beautiful." This word designates the desire of those who search for the hidden beauty of God, or rather of those who search for God, in whom is revealed all beauty. When one turns toward the Good and is linked to the Truth, beauty leads to the One who is the source of it.

The *Philokalia* is first a literary work that describes the environment of the soul in which the great battles of man occur against evil, illusion, and ugliness. This work is an anthology, a *florilegium*, "a collection of flowers," of texts arranged most frequently in short paragraphs, sometimes without any apparent connection between them, making the thought leap from one idea to another, by following a general guideline. It is not so much a question of letting oneself be convinced by the reasoning as it is of receiving a spiritual experience, less of surrendering oneself to an intellectual reflection as it is of making oneself receptive in mind and heart, and of verifying thereby one's own practice by associating with these giants of the mind. Everyone can put together his own *Philokalia* by gathering one's favorite texts in order to return to them at leisure. In the eighteenth century, a long title was given to the collection. According to the prevailing mode, it was at the same time a summary of the content and an outline of a program of action: *The Philokalia of the Neptic Saints Gathered by the God-bearing Fathers, Where One Sees How Through the Philosophy of the Active Life of Contemplation, the Intellect is Purified, Illuminated, and Made Perfect.* The *neptic* Fathers (the word *nepsis* means vigilance, watchfulness) are those who have struggled against a scattering of the thoughts by mounting a guard over the heart.

St John of Kronstadt

Love appeases and relaxes the heart pleasantly, and vivifies it, while hatred contracts it painfully, and troubles it. Those who hate others are their own tyrants and torturers. They are more foolish than fools.

According to the etymology of the term, the Fathers are "God-Bearers" (in Greek, *theophoroi*) for they carry the name they have vowed to pronounce, to enclose it in the prayer of the heart in which God manifests his presence. Finally, then, the term *philosophy* should be understood in its original sense as "love of wisdom," a wisdom turned toward action as well as contemplation.

The first great *Philokalia* is the work of two men, St Macarius, bishop of Corinth, and St Nikodimos the Hagiorite, a monk from Mount Athos. Both had gathered texts by some thirty authors. These texts range from the fourth century writing of St Antony, father of monasticism, to the fourteenth century with St Gregory Palamas, the great Byzantine theologian who was able to make a kind of synthesis of this Christian "philosophy." Greece was then under Turkish domination; hence, the work had to be published abroad in Venice, in 1782. Sts Macarius and Nikodimos wanted to make a contrast between the rationalism of the Age of Enlightenment and of the Encyclopedists that was spreading in Western Europe, on the one hand, with the search for another light, the uncreated light, hidden in God, able to reveal itself thanks to those who persevere in prayer on the other.

About ten years after the publication of the Greek *Philokalia*, a monk from the Ukraine, Païsy Velichkovsky (d. 1794), spent some twelve years on Mount Athos, where, at that time, the authentic practice of hesychasm seemed to have become obsolete. St Païsy then installed himself in the monastery of Neamts, in Romania. Indeed, in the Ukraine, as in Russia, most monasteries were closed by order of Catherine II. The saintly monk gathered together a community of Romanian and Russian monks—the offices were sung in two languages. With some brethren he set about the enormous work of translating numerous patristic texts into Slavonic, the church language of the Slavic lands. It was at that point that there appeared the *Philokalia* of St Macarius and St Nikodimos, which allowed them to pursue their translation work under better conditions. St Païsy did not consider publishing his own translation. According to him, the practice of hesychasm should be reserved for monks in obedience to the direction of experienced fathers who alone can prevent them from getting lost in spiritual illusions. Metropolitan Gabriel of St Petersburg, aware of the importance the work could have in improving the general spiritual climate in Russia that had deteriorated heavily, succeeded in overcoming Païsy's reluctance. He appointed a committee charged with preparing the edition, in 1793, of the *Philokalia*, under the title of *Dobrotoljubje*—this differs from the Greek title, since in Slavonic it means "love of goodness"—and its impact was considerable. It was a copy of this *Philokalia* that the Russian pilgrim carried in his bag. These two works—the Greek *Philokalia* and the Slavonic *Dobrotoljubje*— were at the beginning of the "philokalic renewal" of Orthodoxy, toward the end of the nineteenth century.

In 1877, Bishop (now Saint) Theophan the Recluse undertook a Russian translation of Païsy's *Dobrotoljubje*. He added some modifications to it. In particular, he removed certain texts of a difficult theological nature. He also excised some other texts devoted to the psychosomatic technique that allows one to set the rhythm of the prayer by the breath or the pulse, but which can also cause serious repercussions in inexperienced persons. As such, this *Philokalia* was received favorably by the public. However, important texts, known and loved, did not appear in it. But some had already appeared separately, for example, *The Apophthegmata* (Sayings) of the Desert Fathers, *The Ladder* of St John Climacus—well known in the West thanks to the translation of it by Arnaud d'Andilly, in the seventeenth century—and also the *Treatises* of St Isaac the Syrian—a book Dostoevky loved and a copy of which he placed in the room of Smerdiakov, the "bastard" brother in *The Brothers Karamazov*. In 1917 the Revolution broke out in Russia, and, from the beginning, there was a savage policy of repressing any expression of religious sentiment. A study could be made to find out to what extent the philokalic spirit and the tradition of the Jesus prayer succeeded, somehow or other, in maintaining a flame of the faith where they closed or burned down churches, and even where people lived in gulags.

Through the end of the nineteenth century and during the twentieth, there were other Greek editions of the *Philokalia*. It was translated into Romanian in 1946, and adorned with an excellent critical apparatus by the great theologian, Fr Dumitru Staniloae. In London, England, large philokalic excerpts in translation appeared in 1951, entitled *Writings from the Philokalia on Prayer of the Heart* and then, in 1954, under the title *Early Fathers from the Philokalia*. In France, we have the *Récits d'un pélerin russe* translated by Jean Gauvin, at Lausanne, in 1943, that made the philokalic spirit known for the first time to the French public. In 1953 the *Petite Philokalie de la prière du cœur* was published by Jean Gouillard. With an insistence that is sometimes excessive, this author highlights the "spectacular" aspects of hesychasm, particularly the psychosomatic techniques, while neglecting the necessary implanting in the ecclesial and sacramental tradition. In 1968 the French translation of the Greek *Philokalia* was begun. It was carried out by Jacques Touraille, under the direction of Fr Boris Bobrinskoy, and it appeared in eleven volumes. This translation was taken over by Desclée de Brouwer and published in two heavy volumes. Other translation undertakings, of lesser volume, saw the light of day in Spain, Italy, and Latin America. In this manner, the philokalic spirit reached a dimension of universality. A spiritual father, Jerome of Aegina (d. 1966) recommended "that one should not hesitate to beg, if necessary, to be able to buy a copy of it."

The Art of Arts

Based on the *Philokalia*, hesychasm constitutes one of the paths that lead to the heart of Orthodoxy. Rooted in the words of Scripture, the hesychast tradition goes back to the Desert Fathers, at the time of St Antony (fourth century). This more-than-millenial tradition has never been interrupted in the home of hesychasm, the Egyptian deserts. From there, it spread into Sinai, Syria, the monasteries of Mount Athos, Russia, Greece, the Balkans and finally, in the twentieth century, and thanks to emigrations from the East, western Europe and America. Even though hesychasm has spread in the western sphere, it remains largely unknown there. Viewed as "the art of arts," it represents one of the inner dimensions of Christendom. For one of its commentators, hesychasm designates the path that constitutes "the spiritual axis of Orthodoxy."[1] The range of hesychasm should be expanded. Aside from the monks who, with their own arms, lead the combat of every Christian, there are lay people engaged in life in the world, and belonging to all Christian traditions, who desire by this method, wherever they are, to be servants of the inner peace which only Christ and not the world can give. There exists a "hesychast spirit" that is nourished by prayer, the contemplation of icons, and listening to the words of the Liturgy. It is linked to all the symbols that carry the presence of the divine in order to let this presence then become radiant in the world, even in the humble occupations of daily life. A hesychast monk lived in a small hermitage near a small village that he visisited frequently in the region of Tours. The inhabitants of this village who were not zealous practitioners said of him: he never spoke to us of God, but he always compelled us to think of him—a method that requires tact, and preserves the one thing necessary.

The message of hesychasm and its practice in today's world could bring a contribution, no matter how modest, to in-depth dialogue between the Christian confessions. This contribution is made possible, beyond the theological controversies whose importance should not be minimized, when contemplatives embark on a quest for God in the desire to partake of the divine nature. Here it is not possible to tackle the mystical trends of Judaism and of Islam, which have more than one point of contact with hesychasm. Indeed, on a higher level, all mysticism can meet in the unity of the one God toward whom they tend.

Entering into Hesychasm

At the dawn of the history of hesychasm, St Antony entered a church one day and heard these words that decided his vocation: "If you want to be perfect, sell all that you have, give it to the poor, and you will have treasure in heaven. Then come, follow me."[2] Unlike the rich young man in the parable who does not manage to detach from his earthly goods, the future father of monks, after taking care of some indispensable family

---

[1] Placide Deseille, *La spiritualité Orthodoxe* (Paris: Bayard, 1997), p. 135. In English: *Orthodox Spirituality and the Philokalia*, trans. by Anthony Gythiel (Wichita, KS: Eighth Day Press, 2008), p. 157.

[2] Mt 19.21.

business, since he did not want to harm anyone, distributed his posses-sions to the poor, and then disappeared into the desert in order to lead a hesychast life. When the Russian pilgrim, after losing his wife and his few possessions in a fire, heard these words of St Paul, "Pray unceas-ingly," during the course of a Liturgy, he never stopped until he found a staretz who was to teach him how it is possible to put into practice an injunction apparently foreign to the conditions of human life. Both the father of monks and the Russian pilgrim received an irresistible appeal that emerged from scriptural words they could not escape. This appeal opened to them the path of *hesychia*.

One enters hesychasm as one enters religious or married life or any other creative type of life: with a total investment of one's being. A cer-tain solitude, implied by this state of peace, of silence, requires a toning down of the world's noisy agitation, but this is not at all the equivalent of retreating from the world. When Jesus wanted to pray to the Father, he withdrew to a mountain, and then came down again to the people. Whether he lives in the desert or in an urban building, the hesychast must discover in himself this inner mountain where he can isolate him-self in calmness, where the soul is surrounded by rest, and the inner thoughts and movements are silenced, in a temporary suspension of all activity to render the mind and the heart ready for contemplation.

When Zacchaeus wanted to see Christ, he left the crowd, and as-cended by climbing up a sycamore tree where the gaze of the Lord would cross his. This momentary withdrawal from the world, this contact with Christ, involved a new life choice: he distributed half of his possessions to the poor. When Elijah, after receiving a divine warning, prepared to receive the coming of the Lord, there was first a storm wind that broke the rocks. But God was not in the tempest. Then there was an earthquake that shook the mountain. But God was not in this quaking. Then there was a fire. But God was not in the flames. Finally, there was a soft, light murmuring, the murmur of a tenuous silence. God was there, and he ad-dressed a word to the prophet. It is in this state of silence, of an intangible murmur, that the hesychast wishes to settle. In a world that is saturated with noises, where one's attention is constantly struck by floods of noisy and visual images, the one who has entered hesychasm and has become a bearer of silence allows a new world to be glimpsed. Did not St Isaac the Syrian, already in the seventh century, say that silence is the language of the world to come?

The Goal of the Christian Life

Peter tells us that the highest priced goods have been awarded to us so that we might become "sharers of a divine nature." In light of the words of the apostle, the great eastern spiritual Fathers insist on union with God as the goal of Christian life in order to transform human nature by the energies of the divine Spirit. Since the Incarnation, when God became man, the gap between God and man has been bridged. It can be given to man, within the limits of his own nature, to live the divine life which God had offered him to share in Eden. Christ came to earth to restore this life in him and to reestablish this intimate relationship, interrupted by the Fall. When man partakes of the divine life—it certainly is a question of participation, not of an identity of essence—his essence does not change. He makes a return to his original state. He is deified.

The Russian theologian Vladimir Lossky sees in deification the main difference between the Eastern and Western Churches. He suggests that the Orthodox Church does not know the theme of the imitation of Christ on which the German mystic Thomas à Kempis (d. 1471) wrote a work that had a great impact in Western Europe. Actually, the Gospel certainly invites imitation. At the time of the washing of the feet, Christ exhorts his disciples, "If I have washed your feet… you also should wash one another's feet. I have set you an example that you should do for each other as I have done for you" (Jn 13.14–15). It is true that imitation wants to maintain a certain distance with respect to the person one wishes to imitate. Imitation may be satisfied with purely moral conduct, while true imitation brings into play the union of the deep heart with God. However, it is no less true that the practice of the imitation of Christ in the teaching he gives us, for example, in the Beatitudes, is a sure means of entering into a deep union with him, in the sense in which the Eastern Church speaks of deification, the sense in which Nicholas Cabasilas speaks of "living in Christ."

Hesychasm is first a manner of being and living in God. Would it preach a flight far from the world? Not in the least: if there is a flight, it is only far from the laws of this world. When St Nilus of Sora says that one should not burn heretics but pray for them, he finally distances himself from the laws enacted by men, even when they might be believers. God is at the heart of the world he created. He never ceases guiding, protecting, and saving it. The hermit who chooses a place to live deep in the desert is, according to the words of Evagrius of Pontus, "separated from all and united to all." Prayer establishes a link of communion with all people, whether one is in the desert or in the heart of a city. Arsenius prayed the Lord to lead him on the path to salvation, and he received this answer: "Arsenius, flee from people, and you will be saved": flee from people not because of a spirit of loathing them, which is not at all according to the gospel, but in order to meet them again on a higher level and to make an offering of them to God in prayer. A man whose heart is purified purifies the world that surrounds him, and his prayer creates a barrier against the upsurge of the forces of evil here below. At the time St Antony lived in the desert, the demonic armies amassed around his humble hermitage. Their leader had to ask God to stop this fervent prayer of the monk that threatened to wreck his demonic empire. By contrast, in Alexandria, a single little demon was more than enough to maintain vice in the large city!

There is nothing a hesychast abhors more than to have his meditations interrupted by an unwelcome visitor. Even a bishop learned this at a cost. His name was Theophilus, and he passionately wished to meet a solitary, who then told him: "What I tell you, will you put it into practice?" "Certainly," the prelate said. "Then, do not come near where you learn Arsenius is." Hermits that they were, these Desert Fathers had no equal in unmasking and sending away those searching for the sensational. These men devoted their time to humble manual work such as cultivating a kitchen garden or weaving baskets, for the work of the hands frees the tension of the mind. All his life, Arsenius had remained seated at his work, and on his chest, a wrinkle had been made by the tears that flowed from his eyes. In the island of Porquerolles there is actually a monk who has opted for this type of life, while working to restore an old military fort destined to serve as a place of encounter.

It happens that some solitaries are beset by a strong desire to move, sometimes to flee. The ancients said that, in this case, one should remain in the cell, in silence. The latter will teach them everything they need. The aim of this somewhat enigmatic advice is to stabilize the monk, to prevent him from dreaming about an elsewhere painted in bright colors, an illusion, nonetheless. The cell is the room of the soul, only the one who is at peace with his soul and who supports himself in solitude finds rest in the cell. They said of the cell of a hermit, in which the latter had locked himself out of love for the name of Jesus, "that it is a place of rest; no demon can penetrate there, not even their prince, the devil."

Nowadays people are constantly solicited by multitudes of audible or visual images (television, publicity, the computer, portable electronic devices and phones...) that propel them outside themselves. When silence is brutally imposed on them, for example, at the time of a stay in prison or at the hospital, this can cause true suffering, going as far as delirium. But, conversely, the one who dares descend into his own abyss may encounter the One who is at the origin of everything. Is it not paradoxical to ascertain that a stay in prison or at the hospital, places of suffering, can allow certain individuals to have a decisive experience of inwardness, the discovery of their innermost heart?

Hesychasm is a way of keeping times of contemplation and times of action in a harmonious balance. The Gospel begins a meditation on this theme in the Martha and Mary episode. Jesus does not at all reproach Martha for watching over the good tenure of her house. Mary has chosen the better part, for when the Master is there it is good to stop attending to household cares to listen to his words and contemplate his beauty. The dialogue where Jesus presents himself to Martha as the one who is the resurrection serves to highlight the contemplative ability of this activist of domestic cares. In a generalization which, like all generalizations, sins by excess, Fr Sergius Bulgakov writes that the Catholic Church has received the gift of organizing life on earth and the Orthodox Church that of contemplating the beauty of the spiritual world. Even when it is a question of general trends, the one does not go without the other. "If you are a theologian you truly pray. If you truly pray you are a theologian," Evagrius of Pontus stated, emphasizing by these words how the times of contemplation—praying—alternate with those of action—doing theology. Each comes to the other's aid, with the spiritual experience coming first, then giving place to acting.

Spiritual Fatherhood

Human nature is rather frail. The one who ventures on the road to hesychasm can easily be deluded, letting himself be caught in the nets of illusion. All religions practice a manner of transmitting their message from master to disciple. Now, in the conditions of actual life, it may be rather difficult to find an authentic master, a staretz or *geron* (the Greek term for elder) capable of guiding the novice on his way. A monk, Nicephorus the Solitary, brings elements of an answer in the *Philokalia*:

> Thus, we should look for a sure guide in order to learn from him and to represent to ourselves, by the form of his testimony, the lack of attention that threatens us... and the excesses to which the clever one leads us. Such a guide enlightens us with the experiences he himself has suffered in his trials... If you have no guide, you should take care

to search for one. But if you don't find one, invoking God with a broken spirit and in tears, and beseeching him in your poverty, do what I tell you.[3]

Nicephorus then develops the foundation of his teaching on the prayer of the heart.

To find one's way and make progress, it is necessary to prove one's discernment. In the thought of St Paul, who insists particularly on this point, discernment is a gift of the Spirit, a charism, a "light of the soul" that allows one to find one's bearings in a world of darkness. It is able to verify the authenticity of the spiritual approach, to deepen it, to purify it, and to allow the soul to enter into God's infinite love.

In hesychasm, spiritual fatherhood is essentially non-directing. A young monk asked an elder to take him into his service, and he was surprised to not receive any instruction, to which the elder replied, "I will not say anything. If you wish, do as I do." Obedience cannot be imposed, transmission occurs through exemple. Newly elected to be the head of the community, a monk complained: "They want me to command them." He then received this advice: "Do nothing of the sort. Be a model for them, not a legislator." St Paul wrote to the Corinthians: "I am not the master of your faith, but a servant of your joy."[4] When St Sergius saw his brothers fall prey to dissension, he left the monastery in order not to constrain them by his authority, and to help them mature by themselves. Later, after peace returned, he returned to them.

The danger of words, which are so easy to utter, is that they do not always provide an authentic spiritual experience. As we saw during the events of 1968, our times witness to the representation of fatherhood. It is often a salutary revolt when generational conflict takes aim at a fatherhood that is too authoritarian, but it is often a sterile revolt when the various images of fatherhood are systematically despised (the father, the professor, the policeman, etc.). Perhaps such conflict secretly hides an authentic search for the only Father capable of infinite love. But, buried in silence, he seems to have left center stage. Left to himself, man then wants to live deeply the mystery of freedom. One sees slogans appearing, such as "it is forbidden to forbid," slogans that forget that any freedom has its limits, placed there by God under the symbol of the tree of knowledge. The one who draws his own rules of moral conduct, no matter how

---

[3] *La Philocalie des pères neptiques,* trans. by Jacques Touraille (Begrolles-en-Mauges, France: Éditions de Bellefontaine, 1990), 10: 51.

[4] Cf. 2 Cor 1.24.

generous they might be, always runs the risk of making a god of himself. Wanting to be free can only be a gift of God. Through his disobedience to God, man was chased away from paradise. Through his obedience to the Father, the God-man, willingly divested of his divinity, became the suffering servant. He offered to die on the cross to free the human being from the hold of death.

A question arises. Is *hesychia* possible for lay people living in the world, far from the surroundings favorable to contemplation offered by a monastery or a hermitage of the desert, under the direction of a spiritual father? Asked many times, this question has received contradictory answers. Why not imagine that lay people in charge of a family, committed to life in the world, might settle in silence, arrange for moments of hesychast prayer in their life, and conduct it in the spirit of the ancients? The quantity of prayers is worthless if purity of heart is lacking. When an angel informed the great Antony that a little cobbler in Alexandria raised a prayer received favorably by God, he hastened to visit him and ask him how he prayed. The man replied that, harassed by his job in the evening of his day, he asked God to save all of humanity, in the awareness that only he deserved to be damned. Greatly edified, Antony learned that a humble craftsman can practice *hesychia*.

In imitation of St Antony, who lived as a recluse for several years, numerous spiritual fathers, after a time of fighting against the passions, when their soul had acquired serenity, opened the doors of their cells and welcomed the crowds searching for a word of wisdom or a word of healing. Around St Seraphim, the people pressed in such great numbers that some were sometimes satisfied by merely hearing the sound of his voice that, all by itself, comforted their souls. Certain Fathers had an amazing gift of clairvoyance. St Ambrose, of the monastery of Optina, received so many letters that he could not answer all of them. He spread them on the ground and, with his cane, he pointed out the ones he had planned to answer. Other Fathers, while living as recluses and by receiving no one, nonetheless exercised a spiritual fatherhood by correspondence. Such was the case of Theophan the Recluse, as well as that of Barsanuphius and John[5] in the land of Gaza. Their letters were published, and they are a mine of precious advice on the practice of the spiritual life in the world, advice given by these men devoted to hesychasm. A certain type

---

[5] See *Letters from the Desert, Barsanuphius and John*, trans. by John Chryssavgis (Crestwood, NY: St Vladimir's Seminary Press, 2003).

of fatherhood is always necessary. Only it can maintain self-confidence in an approach that deepens between hearts, to then be engulfed in the heart of God.

The Fight against Death

Frequently translated by the words *serenity, inner peace,* or *impassibility,* hesychasm nonetheless does not claim serenity as a goal in itself, the one goal being union with God. It differs from the Stoic *ataraxia* (detachment), the indifference of Epicureanism, the serenity of a yogi, and the *apatheia* (dispassion) of a Buddhist, detached from the worries of this world or having killed in himself any trace of desire. The Buddha, the perfect type of man who has reached serenity, and whose gaze is entirely directed inward, keeps his eyes half-closed. Christ too wants to be a bringer of peace, but he opens his eyes to people's miseries, and he comes to their aid to heal them of their suffering. Healing is not achieved by a mastery over suffering—reserved for very few people—but by compassion, love, and forgiveness. Any being, even if deeply neurotic, deserves to be saved.

The episode of the Transfiguration on Mount Tabor shows Christ appearing in the splendor of his divine glory, a source of amazement for the three disciples who are its witnesses, and of a feeling of beatitude such as they have never experienced. But in the conditions of earthly life, such beatitude could not be prolonged. The Apostle Peter is wrong when he hopes to remain there by proposing to put up tents. Indeed, one must come down from the mountain, go down into the valley of tears where humanity is lamenting, come down toward cruel people determined to arrest this light-filled being who bothers them, to drag him before a parody of justice, and finally to put him on the cross. For Christ, it is not a question of confronting death like a Stoic, or of breaking the infernal chain of the transmigration of souls, or of announcing the fusion of the soul in a Great Undifferentiated All where the person, as a result of multiple transmigrations, has lost all identity. These ideas of reincarnation strangely benefit from great fashion today, as if they make the inevitable deadline of death recede.

The Christian idea is altogether different. If God comes to earth, it is to fight against death and to free people from its control. The icon of the Nativity represents the divine child laying in a manger in the image of a tomb and wrapped—already!—in a burial shroud to prefigure his last struggle. The victory over death signifies a maintaining of the integrity of the one person, in body and soul, beyond the forces of disintegration. It is the person as such that rises in his flesh—in the biblical sense of the human composite—bearing the stigmata of the suffering felt during life, but not of the suffering itself, as is shown in the episode where Christ tells the Apostle Thomas, "Reach your finger here, and behold my hands… Do not be unbelieving, but believing."[6] Faith in the manifestation of the glorious body beyond one's passing differentiates death in the Christian faith from other religions or from the philosophies drawn up by men.

The serenity of hesychasm does not provide weapons to move blessedly from life to death. For us, Christ has already routed death. The putting to death of death is above all an act of faith. It will be effective on the Day of Judgment when, according to the Apocalypse, the Beast will be thrown into the lake of fire. Serenity is a means to dispose the soul to look for God, for the imitation of Christ, who is "meek and humble of heart."[7] It derives from the spirituality of the Sermon on the Mount in which one can immerse oneself in depth, in solitude and silence. The Christian does not know in what state of mind he will be when his time comes. But he knows that fighting against death consists also in helping those who enter into agony, in surrounding them with one's entire presence, one's attention, one's love, as in this amazing story of the death of a visitor to Mount Athos:

> A group of monks is gathered under the vine in total silence. Some are sitting on the ground; the majority, standing, form a close circle around them. On the knees of the dean rests the head of a mature man, a guest, judging by his garments. The face is pale and drawn, completely abandoned on the stone. The monk tenderly massages his temples, then, with the full palms of the hand, the cheeks, while murmuring words to him which only they are able to understand. The seated monks rub the inert man's hands, slowly, from the elbow to the extremity of the fingers. The man looks peacefully into the air. Sometimes, like a child toward its mother, he turns the eyes toward the monk who holds him against him. Finally, softly passing away, at a certain moment, he no longer looks. They still caress him for some time, then they close his eyelids, and make the sign of the cross over him… They begin to talk; I can hear them saying that this "servant of

---

6 Jn 20.25–27.

7 Mt 11.29.

God" must have been good, for having left so easily... The unknown visitor was dead.[8]

Purification

One cannot start hesychasm if one has not become conscious of a fundamental lack, an inner emptiness, a deep ignorance of the human condition. Only an experience of God can reveal to a human being his sinful condition, can make him be aware that, apart from God, he is nothing. This contrast between man's grandeur and his nothingness is described by St Macarius of Egypt as follows: "The soul is neither of the nature of divinity, nor of the nature of darkness, but she is a creature of reason: magnificent, great, marvelous, and beautiful, 'the image and likeness of God'; and the malice of the dark passions has entered her through transgression."

A large part of the indifference of our contemporaries toward the God revealed in Scripture depends on this ignorance, this refusal to recognize the "sinful," fallible condition of human life. The concept of sin is resented as being ancient history, prehistoric, and most certainly pre-scientific. The multiplication of suicides, of anxieties, of mailaise, issue a scathing denial to our Promethean civilization, proud of its scientific and technical advances, which are indeed real but which account for only a minute part of the mystery of human life.

It is appropriate to first define this malice of the dark passions. The ancients enjoyed making catalogs of vices called *logismoi*—that is: "thoughts"—that come to perturb the psychic life. The hesychast must fight a merciless war against them. One of the most famous catalogs is due to the insight of Evagrius of Pontus, who identifies eight of them. They are the "deadly sins" that lie at the root of all evils, namely gluttony, lust, love of money, sadness, anger, *akēdia* (this word, stronger than depression, designates despair, suicidal despondency), vainglory, and pride. This classical list was imported into the West by St John Cassian. Later, Pope Gregory the Great modified this list and reduced the number to seven.

These evil thoughts, or deadly sins, have been interpreted inappropriately in an exclusively ethical sense. Their misinterpretation lies at the origin of an oppressive morality that has obliterated the message of the

[8] Pavle Rak, *Approches de l'Athos* (Bellefontaine, France: Èditions François-Xavier de Guibert, 1998), pp. 53–54.

good news contained in the gospel. A good Christian—hearsay has it—is one who must do good, while the aim of the Christian life is first to be united to God, so that his will is fulfilled in life: "It is no longer I who live, but Christ who lives in me." In a man so "indwelt" by Christ, morality finds its place very naturally, in full freedom. The reduction of the joyful gospel message to a morality is unquestionably at the origin of the disaffection with the gospel in the contemporary world. Now, the passions described by Evagrius are set at a different, equally dreadful level. They plunge their roots in the dark recesses of the soul. Their evaluation comes under a psychological analysis or a spiritual discernment rather than under a clarification by ethical categories. Let us be satisfied here with giving some indications to shed light on a possible approach for two of them.

At the top of the list comes gluttony, an immoderate love for food, with its counterpart, anorexia, linked to a death instinct. It is through eagerness for food that the first man pounced upon the forbidden fruit, and ate the fruit that brought death in paradise. Eating then is the equivalent of asserting one's autonomy toward God, and of self-deification. With the gluttony for everything that can be eaten, as for everything that can be bought, of everything that can be desired, we are at the heart of the problematic of a consumer society. Man is what he eats, St Paul essentially writes. Only a God could, by offering his body given as food, delete the gluttony at the beginning by substituting for it the eucharistic act.

Another example: lust. The seat of sexual desire is not in the flesh, which is neutral and obeys the covetousness of the mind. It is indeed in the mind. It is not a question of taming the flesh, as they formerly said, but of bringing the mind into line, or rather, setting it at peace. At one extreme, among the swine of the herd of Epicurus, the mind can become carnal, while among the saints the flesh can become spiritualized, as can be seen on the representations of the icons. Lust is a lack of respect for one's own body as well as for the body of the other viewed as an object of pleasure and not as a subject of love.

When the Son of God became incarnate in the world on the eve of embarking on his missionary activity, he performed a work of purification—without which his message might not have gotten through—by repelling the triple temptation of Satan. The Russian novelist Fydor Dostoevsky, who in his literary work explored the infernal dimension of the world, commented on this narrative of the three temptations as presenting a false solution to the three major problems humanity must face: the economic problem (changing stones into bread), the problem of science (throwing oneself from the pinnacle of the temple without being hurt), and the political problem (unifying all the countries of the world, but under the power of Satan). One may also detect in this the three temptations every human being must go through: covetousness, the pride of being able to master the forces of this world, the will to be equal to God through power.

These three temptations of Satan firmly repelled by Christ represent, and in a sense repair, the three stages of the serpent's temptation of Eve in Genesis: "Did he really say you were not to eat?" (the bait of covetousness)—"You will not die" (the desire for immortality by mastery over the world and self-love)—"You will be like God" (to rule the cosmos and pride at the root of all evils).[9]

To put up roadblocks to the foundational passions,[10] the hesychasts advocate abstention from the unnecessary, or even from the necessary, the conversion to the love of God the only Almighty One, and purity of heart to be able to contemplate God. After gaining victory over the foundational passions, one should enter into battle against the thoughts. The hesychasts are called "neptic" Fathers—the word *nepsis* meaning *vigilance*—because they carefully control the thoughts, the mental images that invade the field of consciousness. Like a fortified castle, the heart should be guarded as sentries on the lookout to prevent the enemy—the *logismoi*—from assaulting it.

Tsar Ivan IV had a project of building a spectacular palace. One day, Basil, the Fool-for-Christ, espied him during the course of a Liturgy. At the end of the service, the sovereign asks him, "Where were you?" Basil replied, "I was in church and I have seen that you were elsewhere." "Elsewhere, how?" the tsar replied, cut to the quick, "I was at church." "No," Basil said, "I have seen in thought that you marched on the Mountain of Sparrows where you were building your castle." The tsar admitted that it had indeed been like this and he was filled with fear before a man capable not only of not only of mastering his thoughts, but also of reading the thoughts of others.

When man is no longer the plaything of thoughts that dissipate the unity of his being and frequently torment him, when he can focus his attention when he desires it, he becomes impassible. The little inner movie

---

[9] Cf. Gen 3.1–5.

[10] French *passions mères*.

of thoughts, emotions, remembrances, of everything that weaves the inner framework of life, no longer interrupts his activity. But day and night, vigilance can watch without respite: "I sleep, but my heart is awake."[11] The achievement of creating space in one's heart is not an end in itself; it merely allows God to come to fill this void.

The Light

St Symeon the New Theologian

One night when he had arisen and he had said his prayers to the Lord, behold! A luminous cloud descended from heaven through the half-opened roof of the house, rested on his venerable head, and covered him for several hours. It filled him with an ardent and ineffable love, an unutterable happiness and elation. Then he heard a mystical voice that taught him strange and hidden mysteries. Even when this light disappeared, he found that his heart, in the wisdom of God, overflowed with divine grace. After this time, he did not belong anymore to himself, but the grace of God had enraptured him entirely, had made of his tongue a rapid pen, and of his intelligence a source of divine wisdom. And thus, although he was totally ignorant in profane sciences, he spoke of God like the well-loved disciple, and he devoted entire nights to theology.[12]

It has been given to humans to perceive the divine, uncreated light. What is this light? The sun and the moon enlighten the world with a natural light. Or again, electricity, candles, light us up with artificial light, produced by man. The uncreated light comes from another world, and nothing here below can explain its origin. Those who have experienced the divine light are many: Moses, whose face radiated a blinding light at his descent of Mount Sinai, Elijah on his chariot of fire, the three disciples dazzled by Christ transfigured on Mount Tabor, St Paul struck down on the road to Damascus by a flash of lightning surpassing the sun, and many saints who have had visions of Christ, of the Virgin Mary, of the

[11] Song 5.2.

[12] See Placide Deseille, *Orthodox Spirituality and the Philokalia*, trans. by Anthony P. Gythiel (Wichita, KS: Eighth Day Press, 2008), p. 31.

apostles... For God is light. For Scripture, he is even an all-consuming fire. This experience, granted only to a very small number of men and women, is one of the most amazing aspects of holiness to which a human being may be raised by grace. He then experiences a real foretaste of the life to come. Contemplating the divine life is given only to those who have cleared their heart of its slag, of its opaqueness, and have made it transparent, of a perfect purity. A true *hesychia* then establishes itself, based on a peace and a sweetness that nothing can damage.

How is it possible for someone subject to the laws of this world to see a light that has come from beyond this world? Is this light God himself? But no one is able to see God without dying... How is one to respect the infinite distance there is between man and God? God is beyond the sensory, that is to say, what man can understand through the senses, and he is beyond the intelligible, that is to say, beyond what man can under-stand through his intelligence or his knowledge. From this perspective, the knowledge of God would rather be a new birth, a co-birth, made possible by the emptiness created in us, which God comes to fill with his presence and which, in rare cases, appears as luminous.

This co-birth is an ecstatic union. It unfolds in a rapture of the soul carried away to the summit of joy. This rapture can take on many forms: an enchantment before the beauty of the transfigured world lived by the apostles on the mountain of Tabor, or by the Russian pilgrim crossing the plains and forests where the birds, the trees, all of nature, sing the glory of God; a delight before oneself, transformed by the love of God, as when Paul, in the splendor of his deified being exclaims, "I no longer live, but Christ lives in me."[13] It is an amazement before God who, while he conceals himself in his essence—no one can see God without dying—allows this partaking of his divinity and, in some cases, lets himself be seen in his energies where he is entirely present.

Gregory Palamas made the distinction between God's inaccessible essence and the energies where God fully manifests himself, and makes himself participable. It is through these energies that the process of deifi-cation is brought about, where man is united with God, but is not identi-fied with him. By means of this distinction, he tries hard to maintain the insurmountable distance between man and God in his transcendence. He contrasts identification and real union with God who makes him-self participable in his incarnation, a union so greatly desired by the

---

[13] Gal 2.20.

hesychasts. On Mount Tabor, Jesus, in his earthly body, made his divinity luminous to the gaze of the apostles to whom the grace of this vision was granted.

The word *essence*, which preserves God's transcendence, and the word *energy*, which designates the activity of the Trinity spread out in creation to manifest its love for humans and allow the deifying union, are concepts. One should not tighten the meaning of this too closely in an intellectualizing perspective, alien to the experience of union with God. They attempt to preserve the antinomy, crucifying for the human mind, between God, who is above all things, and the God who becomes incarnate. The incarnate God lets himself be seen and transfigures the people, as is evoked by St Paul: "But all of us, with open face beholding as in a mirror the glory of the Lord, are being changed into the same image, from glory to glory, even as by the Spirit of the Lord" (2 Cor 3.18). What man contemplates, he reflects. On his part, Plotinus said: "If you want to see the sun, become a sun yourself."

How is one "to hasten the day of the Lord," as St Peter asks,[14] and work for the transfiguration of the world and of humankind? With original sin, which deals also with the one committed daily by all people, a moat has been dug between creation and its Creator. This moving away from the center is accentuated in our day-by-day stress, pushing oneself too hard—especially in urban surroundings—breaking up the person in a multiplicity of activities, the abundance of information, and of the images that zap through us. What is needed to find again the path of the "deep me" and of one's inner freedom is to retreat from this hectic rhythm and to re-center on what is essential.

Many utopias have wanted to state arrogantly that they would change life and form a new man. They ended up collapsing, not without dragging behind them a scene of desolation. One does not reform society and, above all, one does not remove violence if the human heart has not been reformed by means of a freely-practiced asceticism. The Lord has bridged the gap separating man and God, first by becoming incarnate in the manger at Bethlehem. It depends on man to walk his part of the way, to fill his part of the gap. The one condition is to consent to follow the humble path of entering into the mystery to know that one is loved, and to receive this Love that alone can overcome in him lust for power and free him from all vanity. Every human being bears a spark of light.

---

[14] 2 Pet 3.12.

It is linked to the other sparks of light and, all together, these can let themselves be set ablaze by this fire that Christ has cast upon the earth. For the *Philokalia,* the task of humanity is to find again this transparency of being, before any manifestation of sin, and to reverse the way that led to Adam's exile. It is to regain in humility the unwaning day, detachment from the material, and to walk the way that leads to the heart. It is there that the Father, unseen, is waiting for his creature.

5

YOU ARE THE HEART OF CHRIST

The Body of Christ

Saving Adam's fallen race, severed from the source of life and enslaved to death, required the decisive action of a God, of a Father toward his son. Only this could mend the ontological wound opened in the creature through separation from its Creator. To the pride instilled by the tempter, "You will be like God,"[1] the humility of Christ replies by his descent to earth under the features of the suffering servant, who delivers himself freely to death. To the demon, whose work it is to create division, splitting up, and isolation, is contrasted the Christ, whose work tends to gather together "the dispersed children of God," to assemble under a light yoke those who are weighed down by burdens that are too heavy.

In the Acts of the Apostles, one reads that "the whole group of believers was united, heart and soul…they had everything in common" (Acts 4.32). In the course of the years that followed the commotion caused by the outpouring of the Spirit on Pentecost, community life and church life mingled for a time, but only a time, in an amazing harmony. Over the centuries, the institution took shape. The river of fire that had set alight the hearts flowed backwards. The laws of life took the upper hand in the banal reality of the everyday. In the history of Christianity, rare were the communities, apart from certain monastic circles, that were able to say that they had lived having only "one heart and one soul."

Thanks to the missionary work of the apostles, Christian communities were founded and the universal church, established in Jerusalem—its original heart—spread throughout the world. The local communities were linked to one another by the ties of faith and love, sometimes through financial assistance like the collections organized by St Paul in

---

[1] Gen 3.5.

Macedonia and in Achaia, "in favor of the poor among the saints of Jerusalem."[2] All communities were linked to Christ in this mystic vision St Paul called "the body of Christ." Christ is the head of this body. In his description of the mystical body, the Apostle insists on the organic unity and the interdependence of its members. They draw their energy from a common source, the divine-human heart of the Savior: "These feet, these hands, are in narrow correlation with the heart," Nicholas Cabasilas writes. And in this heart rests the life-giving Spirit, the source of sanctification for the world.

The mystical body of Christ—with these words, the Church may recognize the name that best defines her—is a divine-human body, both through the human quality of its members, and the divine quality of its head. The communion of all the members with their head within one body leads to a corollary, a state of life dear to the Christian East, that of deification. It is a question of a communication of the divine life to the human being that is brought about by the sacraments: the purifying water of baptism where original sin is deleted; the Eucharist where eternal life is transmitted to those who commune of the heavenly bread and blood of the new covenant. The members of the body are thereby made of one blood with each other by absorbing the blood of the Redeemer. In them, death is overcome: "Just as Christ, resurrected from among the dead, no longer dies and death has no hold on him, so will the members of Christ never know death. How could the members always in communication with a living heart taste death?"[3] On his part, the Russian religious thinker Nikolai Fyodorov (d. 1903) writes that there is only one crime: consenting to die.

Contemplating the Passion of Christ

In the West, there exists an experience of a particular piety lived by St Marguerite-Marie Alacoque (d. 1690), in the small town of Paray-le-Monial in the heart of Burgundy, a region marked today by a strong de-Christianization. This woman received ecstatic visions of the heart of Jesus. She received a mission to spread devotion to the Sacred Heart of Jesus, introducing a contemplative movement to which she gave a

[2] Rom 15.26.

[3] Nicholas Cabasilas, *La vie en Christ* (Chevetogne, Belgium: Chevetogne Abbey, 1960), p. 135. In English: *The Life in Christ*, trans. by Carmino de Catanzaro (Crestwood, NY: St Vladimir's Seminary Press,1974), p. 145.

definitive impetus. The divine-human heart of Jesus then became an object of devotion and fervent adoration.

The century of Marguerite-Marie Alacoque was dominated by the brilliant intuitions of Pascal. This thinker knew how to give to the heart its letters of nobility in a deeply Christian anthropological vision, inspired by his readings of Scripture and St Augustine. However, this century, which was also that of the Sun King, was marked particularly by a severe Jansenist morality, the spiritual center of which was found at Port-Royal. Also, it fluctuated between a certain spiritual aridity and a relaxation of morals in the libertine circles which Pascal castigated. The spiritual trend coming from Paray-le-Monial, which acted on the French territories like oil on troubled waters, brought a breath of fresh air to pious souls. It gave them an exigency of authenticity, a devotional simplicity far from the theological quarrels between the Jansenists and the Jesuits, a demand for contemplation based on a concrete underpinning, the heart of Jesus, the source of all graces, that became an object of a true worship. Basilicas, like the one of Montmartre in Paris, built in 1910, are devoted to the Sacred Heart.

Numerous colloquia have been held on the theme of the adoration of the Sacred Heart. One of the most recent took place at Paray-le-Monial.[4] Such colloquia show that in spite of some hesitation, this spiritual trend remains alive in some contemplative circles of the Catholic Church. The preoccupation of the organizers of the Paray-le-Monial colloquy—"Toward a Glaciating or Global Warming of the World?"—was to provide an answer to the anxieties of contemporary society. The latter has known the dehumanizing undertakings of totalitarian systems; conflicts impacting the whole world; the advent of a post-industrial, mechanized, robotized era marked with the stamp of a promethean efficiency, proud of its own scientific progress, an era when values appear suppressed; [as well as] the humanly humble aspirations of the heart, this secret garden where the human being still preserves the space of an irreducible freedom.

In the Christian East, the experience of the particular piety lived by St Marguerite-Marie Alacoque, captivated by the contemplation of the grieving heart of Jesus, remains unknown. In the liturgical texts of the services of the Lord's Passion, notably of Holy Friday, as in certain

---

[4] The Acts of this colloquium were published as *Pour une civilisation du Coeur* (Paris: Éditions de l'Emmanuel, 2000).

mystical texts, the Eastern Church, which has worked out a rich anthropology of the heart, goes deeply into a contemplation of the tortured body of the God-Man. But it does not give any pre-eminence to this particular organ, as St Marguerite-Marie Alacoque did for the heart. In the East, the general theme is rather that of the descent into Hell to which St Paul makes allusion concerning Christ who "descended to the lower parts of the earth,"[5] or as St Peter wrote, "for the Gospel was preached also even to the dead."[6] The burial of the body of the divine one in agony is represented dramatically without any morbid attitude, during the service called "The Entombment" at the Vespers on Good Friday. The life-sized image of Christ lying in the grave, generally embroidered on a heavy cloth, is carried in procession around the church with songs, to be placed on a support in the middle of the nave. The services take place before this symbolic reconstitution of the sepulcher until the very night of Pascha.

A text from these Vespers details the members of the Lord's body that were physically subjected to insults:

> Each part of your saintly body was desecrated for our salvation: your head was crowned with thorns, your face was covered with spit, your cheeks suffered blows, your lips tasted the vinegar and the gall, your ears heard impious insults... Your members were pierced by nails, your side was opened by the lance. O You who have suffered for us... who bent down to us out of love and uplifted us, almighty Savior, have mercy on us.[7]

In this hymn, the heart is not the object of a particular devotion. "The side opened by the lance" is the deadly blow given to the heart of Jesus to authenticate his death. The contemplation does not dwell on the body of Christ in its human dimension, for he never dispossesses himself of his divinity. Even when desecrated, he remains the bringer of salvation for humanity.

On his part, a great Russian saint, Dimitri of Rostov (d. 1709), no doubt inspired by this view of the bruised body of the Lord during a liturgical service, reacted in his own way: "Oh! What do I see?" A frightening and terrible spectacle... ! The body of my Christ, bleeding, hurt... The side of the one who drew from a rib the helper destined for Adam, our ancestor, is pierced through the heart; today, this heavenly bride-

---

[5] Eph 4.9.

[6] 1 Pet 4.6.

[7] Translated by the author.

groom draws from his side a dear Bride, our well-beloved mother, his holy Church, redeemed by his blood, in order to give birth to a numerous posterity, from blood and water. "The Lord says, 'Knock and it will be opened to you.'[8] Now, knocking is no longer necessary, for the soldier's hand has made a large opening… Here is an open door; each one, according to his wish, can 'go in and out, and find pasture' (Jn 10.9)." The side was pierced by a long and sharp lance, which penetrated deeply, with all its length, up to the very heart, and tore it; it tore the heart… [that is] merciful, and moved by compassion toward human beings in distress: the world tore the heart of Christ, even though Christ loved the world with all his heart. "Formerly, in the desert, Moses struck the rock with his rod, and he made water gush forth; with his iron lance, the soldier struck a rock that was the side of Christ, and at once blood and water flowed out; the water for our purification, the blood for our sanctification; the water for our thirst, the blood for our healing…"[9]

Only the wounded heart of the Virgin Mary corresponds to the wounded body of Christ. The old man Simeon prophesied that a sword would pierce her heart. This would be the sight of her Son nailed to a cross. But the Virgin did not abandon the world. She does not cease pouring out treasures of love on all those who, filled with confidence, turn to her.

Thus, Marguerite-Marie Alacoque and the Holy Friday service in the Orthodox Church form two different approaches to the physical, fleshly person of the incarnate God who delivered up his body to redeem man, thereby giving the ultimate proof of his love.

The Heart of the Church of Stone

In its proper dynamic, the architecture of a stone church offers a reflection of the spiritual world. Entering through the narthex, moving across the nave, and arriving at the end point, the altar, this movement represents the three stages of the spiritual life: purification, illumination, and union with God, or *theōsis*. The holy table, on which Christ dies and rises, is the heart of the church, the habitat where the Spirit rests. Being present everywhere and filling everything, the Spirit has no precise place where it rests. However, there are places where it becomes the agent of

[8] Mt 7.7.

[9] Text translated in Michel Evdokimov, *Le Christ dans la tradition et la littérature russes* (Paris: Desclée de Brouwer, 1996), pp. 122–124.

incarnation, such as the Virgin's womb or even the altar on which the holy mysteries of the transformation of the bread and the wine into the body and the blood of the Lord are celebrated. Adorned with the grace of the priesthood before the holy table, the priest beseeches the Master, in the course of the Liturgy, to make him worthy "to partake of the heavenly and awesome mysteries of this sacred and spiritual table." Filled with humility, he knows that he stands "before the glory of the holy altar" of God.

The bodies of people who died in the odor of sanctity sometimes possess the ability to have the energies of the Holy Spirit radiate beyond death, as is shown by the veneration surrounding certain relics. Fragments of relics are sealed in the altar or sown into the *antimension*, a type of portable altar in cloth on which the priest celebrates the Liturgy, and which has its equivalent in the altar stone of the Catholic priests. These fragments "complete the transformation of the table of stone into a table of flesh." St Nicholas Cabasilas goes so far as to say that "these relics are the true temple, the true altar, while that which is made of hands is an imitation of the real."[10] Placed in the heart of the church, these relics maintain the continuity of the faith and the testimony through the ages. They are a reminder that the Church is founded on the blood of those who wanted to imitate their Lord by giving themselves entirely to him, even to the point of sacrificing their lives. The vital energy issuing from the heart of the God-Man, spread in the relics as in the faithful, reaches the matter of this world, such as wheat, the vine, incense, water, and oil. Thus, the elements of this world are saturated, imbued by the divine energies, in a dynamic that makes them transmitters of the sacraments.

One of the unchanging features of the Orthodox Church is preserving a sense of mystery, and even keeping the sacraments veiled, so as to shelter it from any contamination by this world. After transferring the sacred vessels—the chalice and the paten—from the table of preparation (or *prothesis*), where the oblations were set out with a view to consecration, to the table, the priest covers them with a large cloth, the Aër. Together these represent the tomb of Christ, as is indicated in a prayer that is recited at this moment: "As life-bearing and truly more beautiful than paradise and more brilliant than any royal chamber, your tomb, O Christ, is revealed as the source of our resurrection." The notion of altar-tomb is reinforced in the time between Pascha (Easter) and Ascension when the *epitaphion*—a representation of Christ lying in the sepulcher, generally

---

[10] *Op. cit.*, p. 147.

embroidered on cloth—before which the faithful pray during the days of the Passion, is put on the altar at the moment of beginning the celebration of Pascha. Thus, in an almost physical manner, the reality of the tomb is evoked, the source of the regenerated life, inseparable from any liturgical celebration.

From this holy table, the faithful receive the heavenly bread and cup of eternity, as from the One who loved first. They convey the life in God, which an inspired author has called "the eucharistic heart-to-heart." Then, in accordance with the prophecy of Ezekiel, hearts of stone can be transformed into hearts of flesh, and God can write his law in the people's hearts. Then, the Well-Beloved can engrave "not on tablets of stone, but on tablets of flesh, the hearts, and he will be able to engrave there not simply the Law, but engrave in them himself, the Lawgiver."[11] And when, at the moment of the anaphora the priest utters the exclamation: "Let us lift up our hearts!" the faithful can really lift them at this point when they rejoin the One who has created them.

Let Us Say with Our Whole Heart and Our Whole Soul

When the Lord makes himself present among the people, an ineffable peace is given to them in the form of a benediction: "Peace be to all!" or of an entreaty for the conduct of prayer: "In peace, let us pray to the Lord." St Paul evokes this peace as "the peace of God that surpasses all understanding and shall keep your hearts and minds in Christ-Jesus."[12] An indispensable peace to order the chaos of the soul appeases the confused impulses of the heart; a peace that complies with the desire of God who invites [us] "to lay aside all earthly cares: that we may receive the King of all"; a peace required for the dispossession and the availability of the person faced with the fulfillment of the mysteries...

Unfamiliar to pietistic quietness, to the stasis of being, this peace is not a withdrawing into self, even worse a flight from reality, but an aspiration to turn to action in the world. Once he has become a Christ-bearer in the deep fibers of his being, any member of the assembly, at the invitation of his Master, can open his heart to his brothers and sisters and expand it infinitely in this large world that Christ has come to save. Liturgical prayer cannot be separated from action. As the Liturgy of St Basil says, the eucharistic sacrifice is offered indeed "for the life of the world."

[11] *Op. cit.*, p. 74.

[12] Phil 4.7

For his part, St Maximus the Confessor writes that, where the Eucharist is celebrated, there is "the heart of the world."

The Pierced Heart

In the Gospel according to St John, it is said that the Roman soldiers broke the legs of the two crucified thieves but not those of Jesus, who had already given up the spirit. One of the soldiers pierces his side with a lance, and immediately there came forth blood and water. "He who saw it bore witness, and his witness is true... These things were done so that the Scripture might be fulfilled: 'not one of his bones will be broken.'"[13] And as another Scripture states, "They will look on him whom they have have pierced."[14] These verses from the Gospel according to St John insist on the authenticity of the piercing, [which is] corroborated by the testimony of the Apostle, as well as by Scripture. John wants to give credence to the idea that the God-Man had indeed died in his flesh, and that this death was not, as the heretical Docetists believed, a pretence of death (the word *docetism* is derived from the Greek verb *dokein* meaning "to appear, to seem"). Moreover, this death opens up the mystery of salvation. The water and blood that flow from the Lord's pierced side become the symbols of the two sacraments through which believers must pass: baptism and the Eucharist. Certain commentators place the source of life-giving grace that regenerates humanity in the heart opened by the Roman soldier's lance, an inexhaustible source from which humankind returns ceaselessly to drink.

The heart is linked to the mystery of the blood, of which it is the source. It is thanks to the blood shed by Christ and given in the Eucharist by the outpouring of the Spirit descended at Pentecost that man becomes able to observe the law of the Lord. He becomes a being that loves God with all his heart, and his neighbor as himself. Now, what is blood in its mystical reality, Olivier Clément asks, if not a composite of water and fire, the highest expression of which is that shed by Christ, blood distributed in the Eucharist allowing the people to partake of the life of the Kingdom... The heart appears as this center of the human being where contradictory movements are joined together, when the human being turns away from God in his heart, or when God comes nearer to man and speaks to him in the intimacy of his heart. Thus, at Gethsemane, the

[13] Jn 19.34–6.

[14] Jn 19.37.

heart of Jesus is pierced by the desire that this cup may be removed. But he corrects himself at once: "Yet not what I will, but what you will."[15]

The symbolic thrust of the lance is reproduced in the most realistically possible manner during the service of preparing the oblations which immediately precedes the eucharistic celebration properly speaking. The priest makes a deep cut on the Seal, or "Lamb" that will be destined for the communion of the faithful, while saying: "Sacrificed is the Lamb of God who takes away the sin of the world, for the life of the world and its salvation." Then he makes an incision in the right side of the Lamb while repeating the words of the Gospel: "One of the soldiers pierced his side with a spear; and immediately there came forth blood and water; and he who saw it bore witness and his witness is true."[16] Then he pours into the chalice sufficient wine and a little water.

The Liturgy is a commemoration of past events made fully present in liturgical time. While covering the saving stages of the life of Christ, from the crib in Bethlehem to the ascension and the sitting at the right hand of the Father, the Liturgy dwells on those events that have a particular impact on the salvation of the faithful assembled at church. The knife used by the celebrant for these operations is named precisely the "spear," and it even adopts the form of a spear in its triangular blade. The symbolic thrust of the lance given to the heart of Jesus in a gesture of a striking realism suggests that, in the side wound from which flowed blood and water, it is possible to see the birth of the Church, just as Eve, the mother of believers, was taken from Adam's side.

Jesus was well aware of what was awaiting him in the days when he voluntarily gave himself up to the Passion. He had prepared his disciples for this. He had presented himself as "meek and humble of heart," calling to him those who were burdened and overwhelmed to lighten the burdens under which they groan. The thrust given to the heart of Jesus was a thrust dealt to the divine love, to the immense compassion that gave rise to the coming of God on earth.

It is indeed with a heart full of love that Jesus teaches the crowds, to give them new hope. It is with this heart that he heals the sick, comforts the sufferers, gives his flesh and his blood as nourishment so that those who taste of it might have eternal life, that he voluntarily places himself in the hands of the sacrificers to offer his life as a ransom. It is with this

[15] Mk 14.36.

[16] Cf. Jn 19.34–36.

heart that he dies on the cross and descends to the lower regions to free people from their subservience to death, that he gives his Mother to the Church and allows this Church to be born from the blood and water that flows from his pierced side. The person of a Jesus at the same time meek and humble, compassionate and suffering—and there is no true love unless it is accompanied by suffering—is the divine illustration that the very being of God, and the beauty of the face of the Son in whom the face of the Father is revealed, are entirely molded by this love. Welling up from the divine heart, it is spread through the cosmos. It is through love that God creates the world, through love that he models the creature in his image and likeness, through love that he washes the feet of his disciples, for they should be not submissive servants but friends of their Master. The entire mystery of salvation is recapitulated in the heart of Jesus.

The Heart of Living Water

In the vision of Zechariah the Prophet (Zech 14.8), the day on which the Lord is to come, the living waters that have their source in Jerusalem "will flow half towards the eastern sea, half toward the western sea." Understood literally, through these two seas, the Mediterranean and the Dead Sea, this text aims at the return to the fertility of paradise.[17] However, could one not interpret these two seas as the symbolic places of the Christian East and West, between which—in spite of the divergences and beyond theological confrontations—an impartial distribution, beginning with Jerusalem, is made of the living water, that is, of the gifts of the Spirit?

In the Apostle John, the living water has its source no longer at Jerusalem, this heart of the world, but in the human being, in his/her heart of flesh, which is superabundantly endowed with it to be able to spread outwardly to creation itself and thereby transmit life. "If anyone thirsts, let him come to me and drink. Whoever believes in me… streams of living water will flow from his belly" (Jn 7.38–39), Scripture says. Such a radiating of the Spirit is illustrated magnificently by the words of St Seraphim of Sarov on the inner peace acquired by one person, but capable of saving a multitude of people.

If one wants to regenerate the heart, one should live the gift of the Spirit in sharing, in communion. This work of sanctification can reach

---

[17] *Traduction oecuménique de la Bible* (Paris: Alliance Biblique Universelle—Le Cerf, 1988), p. 777 note *x*.

the world and cause it to be governed by the laws of the Spirit, whose action cannot be separated from that of the Son. According to the expression of St Irenaeus, the Son and the Spirit are the two hands of God. Their activity unfolds in the world with a view to redemption, which has been willed by the author of all things.

St Macarius

The heart governs the entire bodily organism and reigns over it, and when grace possesses the heart, it governs all the members and all thoughts, for it is in the heart that the intellect is found and all the thoughts of the soul as well as its desires; through its intermediary, grace equally penetrates into all the bodily members.

The Spirit presides over the fathering of the Son in Mary's womb. He settles upon him at the time of the baptism in the Jordan and never leaves him until the day when, on the cross, Jesus "gave up the Spirit." The Spirit always accompanies the Nazarene in his travels, inspires his teaching, is involved in the miracles, the healings, the exorcisms, and the acts of raising people from the dead. He is the radiant and active witness at the heart of the mission of Christ in the world. The Spirit that Christ sends to his disciples after he has returned next to his Father is the Consoler, in charge of "teaching all things" to human beings. Pentecost is the sign of the advent in power of the Spirit, whose reign will survive until the end of the world. When the prophet Ezekiel writes: "I shall take you from among the nations and gather you from all the countries, and bring you home to your own land; I shall pour clean water over you and you will be cleansed" (Ez 36.24–25), he repeats the theme of the regenerating water. It regenerates the hearts of those that are "taken" from among the nations and set apart because they refuse to be subjected to the prince of this world. Once cleansed of their filth, such people want to live only according to the laws of the new Spirit whose mission consists of molding, softening the hearts of stone to make of them hearts of flesh. In his dialogue with Nicodemus, the Lord declares that "unless one is born of water and the Spirit, he cannot enter the Kingdom of God" (Jn 3.5). Here there is no metaphor of language, but the expression of a very concrete reality, the re-birth of the new man in the waters of baptism under the influence of the Spirit welling up from the heart. The new person is a person of beauty.

6

THE VISION OF BEAUTY

The human being is as much in need of beauty as he needs bread to feed himself or air to breathe. The theme of beauty already appeared in the word *Philokalia*. This title designates the anthology of spiritual texts by hesychasts devoted to prayer of the heart and whose inner aspirations turn them to this God of luminous beauty. For Dostoevsky, beauty is an enigma, a mystery. It is beauty that "will save the world." It is linked to the good—"For the Lord is good," the psalmist says; linked to the truth—"I am the truth," Christ says, because beauty can then express the very essence of the divine.

The Pure Heart Will See God

Blessed are the pure in heart for they shall see God.[1] In him, the Beautiful will be made manifest in its ultimate splendor. In Scripture, the feeling that God exists lets the Psalmist shout in amazement: "The Lord reigns; he is robed in majesty" (Ps 93.1). In the bosom of the Trinity, the Holy Spirit is at the source of this upwelling of majesty. In it, he represents the hypostasis of the Beautiful. He is the origin and the cause of beauty revealed to the believer. He transforms him/her into his likeness, as can be seen in the faces of the saints, streaming with light. This beauty is the uncreated light of the divine essence. In other words, such a light does not have its equal in the conditions of earthly life, where every light has a natural cause (the sun, the moon) or an artificial one produced by man.

Having a sense of the beautiful, whether by letting oneself be penetrated by its splendor or creating it as an artist, is a way of entering into communion with the Holy Spirit, of apprehending him intuitively. The

---

[1] Mt 5.8.

ancient philosophers, like the authors of Scripture, perceived the unity between light and beauty a long time ago. For Plato, for example, beauty is "the splendor of truth." In all the flaming theophanies related in Holy Scripture, the luminous beauty of the Spirit can be seen: the Burning Bush, Sinai, Elijah's chariot of fire, the luminous cloud guiding the Hebrews in the desert and visible again on Mount Tabor. To a certain number of saints, the Beautiful has allowed itself to be seen, by pure grace. For example, the Mother of God says to St Seraphim, during one of his visions, "This one is of our race," so much had the human element in him been raised to the level of heavenly sanctity. Metaphorically, this splendor floods all the seekers of the divine light. They perhaps may never see it here below in the world of darkness, but it is shown in their heart by a feeling of sweetness, of consolation in trials, of certainty in their trials and errors, of joy in the confidence that animates them. "Seeing God" with a pure heart, is also this.

St Paul writes to the Corinthians that they are "the temple of the Holy Spirit" (1 Cor 6.19); that is to say, starting here below your heart can let itself be enraptured by the Spirit of beauty that lives in you and animates you. Moreover, you are invited to let it radiate around you in the luminous communion of the saints. The splendor of beauty irradiates when light is joined to matter. A piece of coal, dirty matter if there ever was one, glows red and becomes incandescent once put into the fire. This also is true for the human heart, when, in spite of its own darkness, it is in the presence of the luminous proximity of the Holy Spirit. To make the heart shine with an ever greater radiance is long-drawn-out, hard work. The old man is never decisively dead to make way for the new man who, in his purity, "is like a mirror, reflecting the glory of the Lord" (cf. 2 Cor 3.18).

We know that in technical terms the background of an icon is called "light," for it is with light that the artist paints his icon. On an icon, any falling shadow is suppressed. Indeed, shadow and darkness hinder the effect of light. The figures bathe in a transparency, in a pure luminosity. When he tackles the face, the painter begins by applying a dark color. He then covers it with a lighter tint obtained by adding to the preceding mixture a certain quantity of yellow ochre, that is to say, light. Repeated on several occasions, the procedure aims at obtaining a face that is illumined more and more, so that the appearance of a figure on an icon follows a progression that reproduces the growth of light in a person. Likewise also the heart, by detaching itself progressively from the works of darkness, gains in clarity. It acquires an ever stronger luminous intensity.

Truth-Beauty

The pure of heart will see God. Seeing God is letting oneself be invaded by the divine light, letting the Spirit shine in the "deep me", asserting oneself in truth-beauty. Such a vision of God finds points of application in nature, history, art, and the Liturgy.

The human being is linked directly to nature through the intermediary of the body, through the air he or she breathes, through the fruits of the earth and the animals he/she eats. The destiny of nature is mysteriously linked to that of the human being. Once chased away from the garden of delights, man drags with him into his exile nature, which, according to St Paul, "groans together and travails until now in hope that the creation itself will be liberated from its bondage to decay" (cf. Rm 8.21–22). But when man gets up again and gets rid of his "smell of death," as St Paul says, the wild animals become tame. Upon contact with holiness, they regain the peaceful harmony of Eden.

Nature is a living being. Following the example of man, it is called to face up to the majesty of God: "Let every breath praise the Lord." "The heavens declare the glory of God." Nature too is asked to fulfill these missions God has assigned to it. One of the psalms compares the sun to a young bridegroom who, "coming forth from his chamber, will rejoice like a giant to run his course."[2] The heavenly Father himself, Jesus says, feeds the birds, which do not gather things in barns, and he himself endows the lilies of the field with sumptuous garments such as Solomon, in all his glory, never owned. The beauty of the material world and the beauty of the spiritual world are closely interdependent. In the fire of his contemplation, St Isaac managed to see the flame of things...

God acts in history. He directs it on paths that it is not always given to man to understand; his presence enlightens it, and gives it its beauty. In Psalm 90 it is said that "a thousand years in God's eyes are but as yesterday that is past."[3] Thus, history must be considered from the point of view of God, in its globalization, on the axis that leads it from the *alpha* to the *omega*. The myriads of human beings that are its actors, once gathered in a totality, constitute what is conventionally called the "total

[2]   Ps 19.5 [18.6 LXX].

[3]   Ps 90 [89 LXX].4.

Adam." This Adam is the Human Being who, across successive generations, underlies and assures the continuity of history, from the dawn of
civilization to the eschatological era. It is for this total Adam that Christ
descended to earth, even to the infernal regions, in order to proclaim
the Good News of the Resurrection to all, the dead and the living. He
knows each one of its members in a personal relationship with him. Once
someone asked a priest the number of parishioners he had in his charge.
He was taken aback before replying that he did not know anything of
this. Among them were all he had buried, all the living and all those who
would be born. Thus, in his own way, he lived the communion of the
saints in this portion of the total Adam, in the space and time that had
been given to him to live.

The cross erected on Golgotha marks the pivot of history. Through
his death, Christ has freed man from sin. In reality, people share not at all
in Adam's sin, for sin is always personal, committed under the exclusive
responsibility of each human being. But they share the consequence of
it, that is, death. At all times, and following Adam's example, the human
being, by turning away from God to be like him, goes to the end of his
freedom and greedily consumes the fruit of the tree of knowledge. To
those who were sitting in the darkness and in the shadow of death, it
was given to them to see a great light arise. Now the salvation brought
by Christ is proposed not only to those he was able to meet when living,
but also to those who lay in Sheol. On the icon of the Resurrection, one
can see Christ firmly grasping the wrists of Adam and Eve, surrounded
by the cloud of witnesses of the first Covenant, to raise them from their
ages-long sleep.

The Divine Beauty

In its progression, history passes through phases that at times seem
stalled, and at others with accelerated rhythm. The New Testament insists on the concept of fulfillment, of the flowering of time: "But when
the fullness of time had come, God sent forth his Son, born of a woman"
(Gal 4.4). It insists on minds and hearts coming to the maturity needed
to understand the significance of the action of Christ. Christ himself re-
proaches the two pilgrims of Emmaus, disoriented by the crucifixion of
their Master, "their little understanding and being slow of heart to believe."[4] The high point of history is reached when Jesus ascends the cross

---

[4]   Cf. Lk 4.25

in order to strike down, from there, death in the netherworld. He is fully aware of revealing to the people the Father's plan for their salvation. On two occasions, at the beginning of his mission in the synagogue of Nazareth, as well as at the moment he gave up the spirit on the cross, he cries out "It is fulfilled."[5] With these words, Jesus proclaims the completion of the mission for which he had been sent to earth. In his person, he recapitulates the entire range of history. From the highest point of the cross, the beauty of Christ encompasses all of history and illumines it. It gives history meaning and points to its goal. This goal is the Second Coming (*Parousia*) when everything will definitely be brought to an end, and the creature will be reintegrated into the divine life. Only God could lift the ancient condemnation, and return to man his fallen beauty: "The living human being is the glory of God," St Irenaeus superbly states.

For Dostoevsky, Christ is the most beautiful human being the world has ever borne. The beauty of the Father is incarnated and revealed in him. In him, our gaze turns toward the source of light: "Anyone who has seen me has seen the Father."[6] In the creation story, day after day, God looks and exclaims: it is "beautiful" or "good," as one generally translates this word, which can have both meanings. By these words, the Creator reveals his essence, his intimate nature which is to be beauty. In him, there could be no malice. God is the source of the beautiful. He is the Supreme Beauty. Communion with him makes all things beautiful on condition, most certainly, that they be true and that they not make a pact with the forms of nothingness, with the false beauty of the devil. When a being turns to God, everything becomes beautiful. Everything becomes gloomy when one no longer drinks from the source of beauty. Beauty is an act of love. Every artist who in his/her creative activity seeks to express this beauty-truth is united to the one who is the origin of this, though he may not be able to give him a name. The beautiful is indeed the splendor of truth. The creation of beauty is an adventure for which one should be ready to give one's life: "Explore the reason that compels you to write," Rainer Maria Rilke recommends to a young poet who had sent him some awkward poems: "Test whether this reason stretches its roots into the deepest place of your heart; respond frankly to the question

---

[5] Jn 19.30, cf. Lk 4.21..

[6] Jn 14.19.

whether you would inevitably die if the opportunity to write were withheld from you."[7]

Transfiguring the Real

The pure essence of religious art, like that of the icon, could even provide a proof for the existence of God. In a moment of elation, Fr Pavel (Paul) Florensky exclaimed: "There is the Trinity of Rublev; therefore God exists!" The role of the beautiful is to transfigure the real, matter, and to seize an immaterial reality through the material. When Cervantes describes how Don Quixote adorns with all the charms of Dulcinea del Toboso a young and ugly woman under a somewhat exaggerated form (appropriate to the character of his hero), he describes a process of transfiguration. In spite of all that separates them, hearts can be joined in the fires of love, in this case a rustic country woman sees how she is adorned with the seductions of femininity. In this sense, art is a "revelation." It brings to light a reality hitherto unknown.

The vision of beauty presupposes an apprenticeship of sight and a maintaining of the latter in good shape: "The lamp of the body is the eye. If therefore your eye is clear, your whole body will be filled with light. But if your eye is diseased, your whole body will be darkness" (Mt 6.22–23). The eye is the place of encounter of the outer and the inner light, of the light of the world and the light of the heart. All are called to purify the gaze. Struck by the infinite immensity of the universe, where man is but a feeble reed, the psalmist nonetheless exclaims enthusiastically: "You have crowned him with glory and honor."[8] In the end, the ultimate work of art is the human being in whom all the divine art is displayed.

Liturgical worship represents the art of arts. Its aesthetic beauty does not derive from the perfection of its forms—even though a well-trained choir and iconography in the proper style will be welcomed with jubilation. But its beauty derives from the holiness of God. It is this holiness, invoked, besought, that constitutes all the beauty of it. The beauty of the Liturgy is an argument more convincing than dogmas because it expresses an experience, the connection between the visible and the invisible in the sacramental mystery of their unity.

The Liturgy is the place of encounter between heaven and earth, the

---

[7] Rainer Maria Rilke, *Letters to a Young Poet*, trans. by Mark Harman (Cambridge, MA: Harvard University Press, 2013).

[8] Ps 8.5 [8.6 LXX].

temporal and the heavenly. It opens the limits of the earth to the mystery beyond. Formerly, Plato said that "what gives value to this life is the spectacle of eternal beauty." This beauty performs a work of transfiguration. It lifts humanity to an ideal level by providing a foretaste of the Kingdom. St Nicholas Cabasilas says this magnificently: "We go up to the holy table: and there, one finds life at it highest intensity... Jesus Christ transforms the communicant, gives him his personality, and the clay that receives the royal dignity is no longer clay, but is transformed into the substance of the king." Pronouncing the name of God is to make him present. Indeed, for the Semites the name bears the essence of the one it designates. It resounds in prayers; it is unceasingly repeated with love, veneration, fear, joy and wonder, in the entire range of emotions that fill the heart.

As the art of arts, the Liturgy combines all of them in a supreme and sacred expression: architecture, chant, painting, dramatic play, poetry, and light—all are put into the service of God and man to allow them to join one another in beauty. In the church, the people are united in close communion with the cloud of witnesses represented on the frescoes or the icons. During the course of the Liturgy all are gathered, in heaven and on earth, around God's throne in a common praise, and in heralding his mysteries to the world.

Beauty cannot irradiate except from a concrete basis: an icon, bread or wine, oil, gestures... In its symbolic dimension, this support indicates the signified. Even more, it makes it manifest in its reality and makes it come alive. In this sense, consuming the eucharistic species allows one to commune in the divine life, to receive the streaming of the gifts of the Spirit. In this sense, likewise, the icon is a material incarnation of the spiritual world. The prayer uttered before it is addressed not to the wooden board covered with paint, but to the presence of which it is the bearer and which emanates from it. Saturated by the energies of grace, the icons are windows opened to the invisible. The iconographer is a theologian. He "writes" his theology with forms and colors. If man becomes what he contemplates, as Plotinus wrote, the light from beyond that wells up from the icon penetrates into the innermost part of his heart.

Another World

Not all beauty reflects the splendor of what is true. When the truth is dissolved into a lie—an illusion—beauty is inverted into demonic beauty. "How are you fallen from heaven, O morning star, son of the dawn... You said in your heart... I will be like the most High... now you have been flung down to the abode of the dead" (Is 14.12–15). It is in these words that the prophet Isaiah evokes the grandiose fall of the angel light-bearer, this Lucifer, the angel closest to God, bathing in his luminous radiance. The possibility of denial, a refusal to serve the one who had placed him so close to himself in order to usurp his place and to be "like the most High," mysteriously, appeared to him.

With the fall of the angel, and in its wake, the fall of man, the world found itself surrendered to the Beast. Evil is unleashed in wars, acts of cruelty, injustices, innocence trampled upon, ugliness, and in the weight of misfortune that beats down on human beings. Evil is what is not conformed to beauty-truth and beauty-love. Now, beauty-truth, even when it is forced to stay in the background, leaves in the soul a longing for another, more beautiful, ideal world. To many minds, this world provokes a radical dissatisfaction with respect to the state of things here below. Such a dissatisfaction exists, whether it preserves vestiges of an ancient paradisiacal past—the myth of the golden age, that charmed the poetic dreams of Virgil—or whether it be projected into a future equally paradisiacal—the millenarianism of the Apocalypse or such totalitarian ideologies haunted by the idea of an earthly paradise. Paradoxically, evil is the best proof for the existence of God. As by an effect of refraction, because Lucifer would not be able to throw a veil of darkness on all things, the very existence of a world subjugated to adversity is the best proof that another world exists, one where truth-beauty is not scoffed at.

Evil is a challenge the Christian is called to pick up without fear of having to cross swords. Christ likes to prepare his disciples to join this fight: "Blessed are you, when men shall revile you, and persecute you, and shall say all manner of evil against you falsely, for my sake" (Mt 5.11). How can one keep a pure heart in a world where women and children are sexually assaulted, where two-thirds of the planet suffer hunger, and the remaining third suffers from over-eating? How can one keep a pure heart in a world where the reign of Mammon, financial corruption, displays its influence everywhere, where unbridled eroticism is set up as a value to the effect that the young involved in "rotations" (collective rapes) consider their acts as normal, where movies of violence and sadism end by damaging many psyches already frail at the outset? It is very serious to see the line between good and evil, between the real and the unreal, become blurred. It is nonetheless in this world that Christ always offers himself as a sacrifice and sends his Spirit to reveal all things. On the eve of the Passion, after announcing Peter's denial, at the moment that history became crazy accelerates its rhythm, Jesus tells his disciples: "Let not your heart be troubled."[9] This is ineffable peace before the upsurge of the waves. This peace allows one to ward off any contamination by the prince of this world. Through this peace, the hearts keep their purity.

To fight against any form of corruption, it would not be reasonable to dream of a return to a morality of triumphalism. Morality does not triumph. It can only be presented as a value and be freely accepted. To return to Victorian Puritanism or austere Jansenism is not possible. Their virtues—and they had them—no longer seduce. Without beauty, the good is neither attractive nor convincing. Without astonishment able to turn the heart upside down, the good loses its power of attraction. It is in this spirit that Dostoevsky lets one of his characters exclaim: "Beauty will save the world." In the midst of the collapse of virtues, salvation resides in the efflorescence of the beautiful before which one can be enraptured in silence. For this, one must go down to the root of things and find a divine seed, penetrate into the essence of things and encounter there the presence of the Creator. A saying of the Desert Fathers states: "After God, see God in every human being."

Creation should be taken into account in its totality, because it is called to salvation in its totality. It is not a question of minimizing the devastating activity of the prince of this world, but of overcoming the current contrast between God and the world, flesh and the spirit, time and eternity. These categories fall under a theology that has not solved the irritating problem of duality. In this theology, the world distances itself from God and separates itself from him. It becomes "secularized" and duality becomes a principle of unbelief. Now, the great events that have Christ at their origin, the Incarnation, the Resurrection, the Transfiguration, provide an answer to duality and transcendence. These events that have a dogmatic value attest that heaven and the world meet, the human and the divine are united, and that eternity comes to intersect time. Being present everywhere, the Holy Spirit fills everything with his unique beauty.

The encounter between the two worlds, divine and terrestrial, permeates the icons with an atmosphere of joy in striking colors. A solemnity that is sometimes austere comes to mitigate such joy, when the heart feels distress when faced with human suffering. Thus, on the icon of the

---

[9] Jn 14.1.

Nativity, the Mother stretched out in a royal purple is this woman of which the Gospel speaks. She feels joy because a man has come to earth. But she also feels an infinite sadness that causes her to turn away from her son who is—already—laid down in a manger-tomb. Soon, Simeon predicts to her that a sword will pierce her heart. She contemplates Joseph, grappling with the tempter, which is his share in the perfect sacrifice which his adoptive son prepares to make. He deserves being consoled by the Angel: "Do not be afraid to take Mary as your wife."[10] And he submits.

The icon called the Holy Trinity by Andrei Rublev enjoys a sure fame in the West. One frequently forgets that it was painted during one of the most tragic periods of Russia's history, that of the Tatar invasions that went on for two centuries. The cruel riders with the slanted eyes looted, killed, raped brazenly, pushing the fearful populations to hide in the forests to protect themselves. It is a miracle that the icon painters at this time painted with a spiritual depth, a delicate touch, a sense of bright colors that remain without equal. They had seen hell. Instead of sinking into despair, they paradoxically had seen that this hell was shot through with dazzling views that announced another world, a world of light and love. Their paintings were steeped in the crucible of suffering.

Security, the comfort of existence, comes later, and so does the meanness born from material prosperity. The icon becomes drab, is saturated with a falsely realistic sentimentality, and falls into decadence. By contrast, the painters of the fourteenth and fifteenth centuries highlight the healing power of beauty because they have reached the bottom of the abyss of ugliness. In his film, *Andrei Rublev*, the moviemaker Andrei Tarkovski transposes this process of the discovery of beauty in the episode where a young boy shows that he is able to cast a bell with a very clear sound. The boy was able to discover the secret of the art carried away by the death of the men of this art—his father had been killed by cholera—which should be interpreted symbolically as the Bolshevik torment. Such is the power of the transfiguration of beauty: it allows one to get back in touch with love, to reconstruct the community of people where the hearts beat in unison. As the biographer of St Sergius writes, the saint had wanted to found his monastery in honor of the Holy Trinity "so that the sight of the Holy Trinity might overcome the fear of the heart-rending division of the world."

[10] Cf. Mt 1.20.

"The Church is one," a Russian theologian of the nineteenth century said.[11] One, for the body of Christ could not be divided. Consequently, there is one body, but it is torn asunder and, without knowing it, the entire world suffers from this wound. Beyond theological controversies, which are always necessary since Scripture asks us to have "an understanding heart," we have to rediscover the path of our common heart. Christ has made manifest this common heart by his death for all people and in his resurrection through the victory over the powers of darkness. "Opening one's heart"—would this then not be entering into communion with all the disciples of Christ, perhaps even with the believers of all religions, and perhaps also with all people, in order to heal the wounds from the rupture from which the world suffers so much?

[11]   Aleksei Khomiakov, *The Church is One* (London: Fellowship of St Alban and St Sergius, 1968).

.

Select Bibliography

Behr-Sigel, Elisabeth. *The Place of the Heart: An Introduction to Orthodox Spirituality*. Trans. by Fr Stephen Bigham. Crestwood, NY: St Vladimir's Seminary Press, 2012.

Bruguès, Jean-Lous, Bernard Payrous, and Communauté de l'Emmanuel. *Pour une civilisation du cœur: Vers la glaciation ou le réchauffement du monde. Actes du Congrès de Paray-le-Monial.* Éditions de l'Emmanuel, 2000, p. 343.

Chariton of Valamo, Archimandrite. *The Art of Prayer.* An Orthodox Anthology. London: Faber, 1966.

Le Cœur. Études Carmélitaines. Paris: Desclée de Brouwer, 1950, p. 402.

Evdokimov, Michel. *Le Coeur dans la tradition orientale et dans les penseés de Pascal.* Contacts 101 (1978): 36–51.

Kadloubovsky, E. and G.E.H. Palmer. *Writings from the Philokalia on Prayer of the Heart.* London: Faber, 1951.

Melloni, Javier. *Les chemins du cœur, La connaissance spirituelle dans la Philocalie.* Paris: Desclée de Brouwer, 1995, p. 174.

Nikodimos of the Holy Mountain and Makarios of Corinth. *Philokalia, The Complete Text.* Trans. by G.E.H. Palmer, P. Sherrard, and K. Ware. London: Faber & Faber, 1984. (See the Index, vol. III, s.v. heart.)

Špidlík, Tomáš. *The Art of Purifying the Heart.* Sapientia, 2010.

————. *The Spirituality of the Christian East.* Vol. 2, trans. by Anthony P. Gythiel. Cistercian Studies Series no. 206. Kalamazoo, MI: Cistercian Publications, 2005, pp. 496–497. (See the Index, s.v. "heart" in Topical Index. See also Topical Index of Vol. 1, trans. by Gythiel (no. 79, 1986), p. 447.)

Spyridon, Logothethis, Archimandrite. *The Heart. An Orthodox Christian Spiritual Guide.* Nafpaktou, Greece: Holy Transfiguration of Our Savior Jesus Christ Monastery, 2001.

Vlachos, Hierotheos, Archimandrite. *Orthodox Psychotherapy: The Science of the Fathers.* Trans. by Esther Williams. Lakesia, Greece: Birth of the Theotokos Monastery, 1994.

Zacharias, Archimandrite. *The Hidden Man of the Heart (1 Peter 3:4): The Cultivation of the Heart in Orthodox Christian Anthropology.* Essex, UK: The Stavropegic Monastery of St John the Baptist, 2008.

INDEX OF NAMES